ASPATORE BOOKS

About Aspatore Books
Business Intelligence From Industry Insiders
www.Aspatore.com

Aspatore Books publishes only the biggest names in the business world, including C-level (CEO, CTO, CFO, COO, CMO, Partner) leaders from over half the world's 500 largest companies and other leading executives. Aspatore Books publishes the Inside the Minds, Bigwig Briefs, ExecEnablers and Aspatore Business Review imprints in addition to other best selling business books and journals. By focusing on publishing only the biggest name executives, Aspatore Books provides readers with proven business intelligence from industry insiders, rather than relying on the knowledge of unknown authors and analysts. Aspatore Books focuses on publishing traditional print books, while our portfolio company, Big Brand Books focuses on developing areas within the book-publishing world. Aspatore Books is committed to providing our readers, authors, bookstores, distributors and customers with the highest quality books, book related services, and publishing execution available anywhere in the world.

The *Bigwig Briefs* Series
www.BigwigBriefs.com

Bigwig Briefs features condensed business intelligence from industry insiders and are the best way for business professionals to stay on top of the most pressing issues. There are two types of *Bigwig Briefs* books: the first is a compilation of excerpts from various executives on a topic, while the other is a book written solely by one individual on a specific topic. *Bigwig Briefs* is also the first interactive book series for business professionals whereby individuals can submit excerpts (50 to 5,000 words) for upcoming briefs on a topic they are knowledgeable on (submissions must be accepted by our editorial review committee and if accepted they receive a free copy of the book) or submit an idea to write an entire Bigwig Brief (accepted ideas/manuscripts receive a standard royalty deal). *Bigwig Briefs* is revolutionizing the business book market by providing the highest quality content in the most condensed format possible for business book readers worldwide.

About Big Brand Books

Big Brand Books assists leading companies and select individuals with book writing, publisher negotiations, book publishing, book sponsorship, worldwide book promotion and generating a new revenue stream from publishing. Services also include white paper, briefing, research report, bulletin, newsletter and article writing, editing, marketing and distribution. The goal of Big Brand Books is to help our clients capture the attention of prospective customers, retain loyal clients and penetrate new target markets by sharing valuable information in publications and providing the highest quality content for readers worldwide. For more information please visit www.BigBrandBooks.com or email jonp@bigbrandbooks.com.

BIGWIG BRIEFS

BIGWIG BRIEFS:
HUMAN RESOURCES & BUILDING A WINNING TEAM

Industry Experts Reveal the Secrets to Hiring, Retaining Employees, Fostering Teamwork, and Building Winning Teams of all Sizes

ASPATORE BOOKS

Published by Aspatore Books, Inc.
For information on bulk orders, sponsorship opportunities or any other questions please email store@aspatore.com. For corrections, company/title up1 dates, comments or any other inquiries please email info@aspatore.com.

First Printing, November 2001
10 9 8 7 6 5 4 3 2 1

Copyright © 2001 by Aspatore Books, Inc. All rights reserved. Printed in the United States of America. No part of this publication may be reproduced or distributed in any form or by any means, or stored in a database or retrieval system, except as permitted under Sections 107 or 108 of the United States Copyright Act, without prior written permission of the publisher.

ISBN 1-58762-015-4

Library of Congress Card Number: 00-110992

Bigwig Briefs Editor, Ginger Conlon

Cover design by Rachel Kashon, Kara Yates

Material in this book is for educational purposes only. This book is sold with the understanding that neither any of the interviewees or the publisher is engaged in rendering legal, accounting, investment, or any other professional service.

This book is printed on acid free paper.

Special thanks also to: Ted Juliano, Tracy Carbone, and Rinad Beidas

The views expressed by the individuals in this book do not necessarily reflect the views shared by the companies they are employed by (or the companies mentioned in this book). The companies referenced may not be the same company that the individual works for since the publishing of this book.

ASPATORE
BUSINESS REVIEW

The Quarterly Journal Featuring Exclusive Business Intelligence, Research & Analysis From Industry Insiders

Enabling Executives to Innovate & Outperform

The Most Subscribed to Publication of its Kind By C-Level Executives From the World's 100 Largest Companies

Only $1,090 a Year for 4 Comprehensive Issues

Aspatore Business Review brings you the most important, condensed business intelligence from industry insiders on a range of different topics affecting every executive, expanding your breadth of knowledge and enabling you to innovate and outperform.

Aspatore Business Review is the only way for business professionals to keep their edge and stay on top of the most pressing business issues. Each *Aspatore Business Review* features business intelligence, research and analysis from C-Level (CEO, CTO, CMO, CFO, Partner) executives, venture capitalists, investment bankers, lawyers, and analysts from the world's largest companies. Each quarterly issue focuses on the most pressing business issues, trends, and emerging opportunities in the marketplace that affect every industry in some way or another. Every quarter, *Aspatore Business Review* focuses on topics that every business professional needs to be aware of such as:

- Staying Ahead of Changing Markets
- Profiting in a Recession/Market Upswing
- Emerging Market Opportunities
- New Legal Developments
- Investment Banking Perspectives
- Management and Leadership
- Fostering Innovation
- Brand Building
- Economy Trends
- Stock Market Outlook
- Technology and the Internet
- Venture Capital Perspectives

Aspatore Business Review is the one publication every business professional should read, and is the best way to maintain your edge and keep current with your business reading in the most time efficient manner possible.

Fill Out the Order Form on the Other Side or Visit Us Online!
www.Aspatore.com

ASPATORE BUSINESS REVIEW
Tear Out This Page and Mail or Fax To:

Aspatore Books, PO Box 883, Bedford, MA 01730
Or Fax To (617) 249-1970

Name:

Email:

Shipping Address:

City: State: Zip:

Billing Address:

City: State: Zip:

Phone:

Lock in at the Current Rates Today-Rates Increase Every Year
Please Check the Desired Length Subscription:

1 Year ($1,090) _____   2 Years (Save 10%-$1,962) _____
5 Years (Save 20%-$4,360) _____   10 Years (Save 30%-$7,630) _____
Lifetime Subscription ($24,980) _____

(If mailing in a check you can skip this section but please read fine print below and sign below)
Credit Card Type (Visa & Mastercard & Amex):

Credit Card Number:

Expiration Date:

Signature:

Would you like us to automatically bill your credit card at the end of your subscription so there is no discontinuity in service? (You can still cancel your subscription at any point before the renewal date.) Please circle: Yes   No

*(Please note the billing address much match the address on file with your credit card company exactly)

Terms & Conditions

We shall send a confirmation receipt to your email address. If ordering from Massachusetts, please add 5% sales tax on the order (not including shipping and handling). If ordering from outside of the US, an additional $51.95 per year will be charged for shipping and handling costs. All issues are paperback and will be shipped as soon as they become available. Sorry, no returns or refunds at any point unless automatic billing is selected, at which point you may cancel at any time before your subscription is renewed (no funds shall be returned however for the period currently subscribed to). Issues that are not already published will be shipped upon publication date. Publication dates are subject to delay-please allow 1-2 weeks for delivery of first issue. If a new issue is not coming out for another month, the issue from the previous quarter will be sent for the first issue. For the most up to date information on publication dates and availability please visit www.Aspatore.com.

BIGWIG BRIEFS:
Human Resources & Building a Winning Team

Contents

Jeff Sheahan, Egghead, CEO	
Be a Leader	13
Jonathan Nelson, Organic, CEO & Cofounder	
Finding Leaders	18
Joe Kraus, Excite, Founder	
How to Retain Top Employees	19
Kyle Shannon, Agency.com, Cofounder	
The Biggest Challenges in Retaining Employees	21
Stephen Andriole, Safeguard Scientifics, CTO	
Recruiting Must be a Core Competency	23
John Ferber, Advertising.com, Cofounder	
The Right Size Marketing Staff	24
Mark DelVecchio, eWanted.com, VP Marketing	
The Makings of a Marketing Team	24
Joseph Howell, Emusic.com, CFO	
Hire Risk-Takers	26
Lynn Atchison, Hoovers, CFO	
Know Your Prospective Employer	27
Using Options as Compensation	27
Tim Bixby, LivePerson, CFO	
The Importance of Money	28
What Prospective Employees Should Know About Internet Companies	28
Louis Kanganis, Nerve.com, CFO	
Rules for Joining an Internet Company	29
The True Value of Stock Options	29
David Henkel, Agillion.com, CFO	
Skills Needed at the Top	30
Keeping the Right People	31

Designing a Fair Compensation Package	33
Who Needs Middle Managers	34

Alan Breitman, Register.com, CFO
Know the Financial and Business Fundamentals	35
Stock Up on Stocks	37

Joan Platt, CBS MarketWatch, CFO
The (Un)Changing Role of Stock Options	38

Mary Dridi, WebMethods, CFO
The Financial Side of Hiring	39

John Somorjai, Keen.com, VP Business Development
How to Establish Goals	44

Todd Love, yesmail.com, Senior VP Business Development
Measuring Success	45

Chris Dobbrow, Real Names, Senior VP Business Development & Sales
How to Build a Business Development Team	47

Daniel Conde, Imandi.com, Director of Business Development
Diverse Skills Sets Make a Team	48

Bernie Dietz, WebCT, VP Business Development
Use Your Contact Network	50

Mark Bryant, LifeMinders.com, VP Business Development
Have the Right Hiring Process	51

Robin Phelps, DigitalOwl.com, VP Business Development & Cofounder
Build a Team Whose Members Have Diverse Skills	52

Andrew Wolfe, SONICblue, CTO
The Makings of a CTO	53
Building a Solid Technology Team	55

Neil Webber, Vignette, Cofounder & CTO
The Role of the CTO	57
The Basis for Building a Technology Team	58

Dwight Gibbs, The Motley Fool, Chief Techie Geek
How the CTO Fits Within a Highly Technical Organization	59
How to Foster Creativity in a Large Tech Team	63
What it Takes to Become a Leader	65

Peter Stern, Datek, CTO
Finding Top Tech Staffers Who Fit the Team	66

Warwick Ford, Verisign, CTO
Interacting With the CEO	68
How Reputation Attracts Stars	68

Ron Moritz, Symantec, CTO	
Balancing New Staff With Veterans	69
Dermot McCormack, Flooz.com, CTO & Cofounder	
Who Is in Demand	70
Pavan Nigam, Healtheon, Cofounder	
Balancing Two Disparate CTO Roles	71
Integrating Technologies From Acquisitions	73
Michael Wolfe, Kana Communications, VP Engineering	
Breadth of Knowledge Versus Depth of Knowledge	75
Daniel Jaye, Engage, CTO & Cofounder	
The Varying Roles of the CTO	77
Key Skills to Look for in a Tech Candidate	77
Gordon Caplan, Esq., Mintz Levin Strategies	
The Most Important Components of an Employment Contract	78
Bonnie Hochman & Harrison Smith, Krooth & Altman	
Basics of the Employment Relationship	80
Interviewing and Hiring	81
The Importance of Properly Screening Applicants for Employment	81
Discrimination in the Hiring Process	82
Non-Competition and Non-Disclosure Agreements	84
Unethical Recruiting (and Anti-Solicitation Agreements)	86
Employment	86
Employment-at-Will	86
Provisions to Include in Employment Agreements	87
Employee Handbooks and Their Impact on Employment-at-Will	87
Family and Medical Leave Act Requirements	89
Termination of the Employment Relationship	90
Termination of the At-Will-Employment Relationship	91
Termination of Employees With Employment Agreements	91
Termination of the Employment Relationship Through Constructive Discharge	92
Limitations on the Right to Fire	93
Issues You Should Consider Upon the Termination of the Employment Relationship (By You or the Employee)	95
Conclusion	99

BIGWIG BRIEFS: HUMAN RESOURCES & BUILDING A WINNING TEAM

Jeff Sheahan, Egghead, CEO

Be a Leader

My area of expertise is management. My career and the success I've had in my career have been due to my ability to lead and develop people, get them to believe in an idea, and get them to communicate the company's strategy and direction. One of my strengths, that has enabled me to do well in my career, is that I work well in a team environment and a collaborative environment. My success has been due to my ability to get folks excited and passionate about delivering great service. I've been able to make the company into something that everyone can be proud of. I've always had to stay current on my understanding of what's going on in my industry and the technology side, but that's become less critical to me in my personal success. It's been more my ability to lead, manage, and communicate. Those are the things that have undergone the most change and evolution for me over the past 20-plus years. I've had to adapt to changing work styles. Certainly working here in California is different than working on the East Coast. Here managers need to be a little more nurturing with people. On the East Coast managers can be a bit more direct. Managers have to adapt themselves, they have to be a little bit of a chameleon and be able to work with a variety of different folks and get the most out of each them. Don't make them homogeneous. Revel in their diversity, but get them all pulling in the same direction. That's the thing I've focused more on in my career, how to continue to evolve and develop my leadership and managerial skills.

In the late 1980s and early 1990s I was a big disciple of Tom Peters' book *Learning to Love Change and Thriving on Chaos*. I used to bring that book out all the time. Whenever I had a new opportunity or I went into a new area or was getting involved in a new responsibility I always brought that out and took folks through it. The first thing people have to recognize is that business is about constant change. They need to recognize that so they don't fight change.

I don't mind working in a world of ambiguity for a while. Some folks can't handle ambiguity. The period between big changes sometimes is ambiguity and there isn't a clear way forward. The thing I recognized, particularly in business, is that people have to change. People have to reinvent themselves every few years. The dynamics of the marketplace are constantly changing, so people can't sit still. What worked five years ago won't work today. The ad campaigns have to remain fresh, the services companies provide the customer need to continually be updated and adapted to what customers are looking for.

The most important thing someone can do is to have her ear to the ground. Listen to customers, particularly in a business like ours, which provides a service. Listening to customers is the number one way that companies can get ahead of change so that it doesn't surprise them. The second is to listen to employees. Third, managers need to be voracious readers and absorbers of information and trends. They need to be aware of what is going on and be attentive listeners. One of the key things that managers can do is to adapt to change. If they really listen to the signs that say change is necessary, then packaging all of that into an understandable change event or shift for their people is crucial. It's an attitude that changes part of life. All of a sudden you calm down, because it's not a cataclysmic event, and then you realize that you know you're going to have to change and continually adapt.

Managers need to look at all the information sources around them and try to get as much information on hand as possible. Then pull that together as swiftly as possible and let people know why the change is occurring and why they're moving the company in a new direction. That last part is crucial. If managers don't have folks coming along with them, then they won't be successful in adapting the business to whatever change is necessary.

The hardest part of the job is recruiting and retaining folks. I always start with open and honest communication. You never lose when you're open and honest with people. One of the hallmarks of my style and the folks who I try to hire and the way I deal with the folks who report to me is an open and honest line of communication. I like to have regular meetings with people, sit down and make sure we're on top of things together. I don't like to let things drift. Folks will gravitate towards an environment in which there's honesty, high ethics, and high principles. That's a real big issue with me. There's no room in life or in business for deceptive practices. We're going to be above board. We're going to hire people who are above board. We try to find folks who rally around those kinds of principles and philosophies and really live those every day.

The other thing managers should do is to challenge people. Folks need to be intellectually stimulated. The only thing that gets them up and out of bed every morning is challenge, something intellectually stimulating about the work that they're doing. Of course, if someone is an accounts payable clerk, processing data, then there's a limit to how much stimulation a manager can provide. But even in that type of a role, managers have to look for a way to give that individual another challenge. Ask him to do something a little bit extra. Give him an opportunity to step out of the work he's doing every day and see if he has the capacity to grow. Managers need to coach and develop people and give them a chance to express themselves in another way. Recognize that most people want to be intellectually stimulated at work. If managers provide outlets for that intellectual stimulation and those opportunities, then they can do a great job of holding on to people. In the end, managers have to have a good strategy for their business to perform.

It's interesting to rank the reasons people leave. Generally, the first reason is that they don't like their boss. It usually comes down to the fact that it's not that they don't like the person, it's that they haven't been communicating well with them. They don't quite know what their goals are, they haven't been given regular feedback, or the person is aloof.

I've learned that top executives really have to work with their middle management people to get them to nurture and develop folks. The other big reason folks leave is that there's so much hype that "this is a new place" and "that's a new place." If a manager has not articulated the company's strategy and mission, then the business has not shown that individual what they're doing. If a manager can make that line very clear, then folks will understand that they're working on projects that are feeding into the goal, which is helping the strategy push forward. If an executive can do that throughout the organization and if she can spend time doing that through quarterly briefings, regular meetings, and feedback, then folks will feel that they're really contributing. That's when folks will stay and folks will feel good about what they're doing.

Recruitment is really tough, especially here in the Valley. We've recently moved some of our operations north to Vancouver, Washington, because we needed to get into an environment where we could have an easier time recruiting and where retention wasn't as challenging. There are some particular pressures here in the Valley, because there are so many new opportunities. The workforce today is a lot less loyal than it used to be and I don't mean that disparagingly. Folks put a year or two in and then they say, "It's time for me to move over here." Before, people tended to work and develop careers in one or two places and then moved on. That goes back to what I said before, managers have to provide folks with a lot of intellectual stimulation. Today's younger people will get bored quickly and managers have to challenge them.

Jonathan Nelson, Organic, CEO & Cofounder

Finding Leaders

We're always looking for great leaders. We're a people business and people who have vision and leadership capabilities are really hard to find, whether that is in the creative group, in the strategy group, or in the technology group. People who really get it are going to be leaders.

In any business there are certain skill sets that are hard to recruit, like engineers, particularly database engineers, and so forth. These people are hard to find, but ultimately it's really a matter of looking for great leaders, people who are really going to build a business.

I've been accused of being a leader and not being a leader many times, and it's too hard and too painful to dissect one's own personality. When I look at leadership, I look at people who, first of all, have integrity, honesty that really comes through, and intelligence, and seem to know what they're doing. Second, they have some charisma and people want to gravitate to and be led by this person. Third is intelligence; leaders have to have a batting average that's pretty high—they have to be making at least four out of five decisions correctly and be validated by the marketplace. Otherwise, even if they have the most charisma and great leadership qualities, people aren't going to be following them, because they're going to be leading them over a cliff over and over again.

The key thing is to have respect and recognition that sets in and stays. A person may appear to have leadership and charisma, but that person has to have integrity and intelligence. That's what makes great leaders.

They also need to believe in what the company is doing. Ultimately it's about peer groups and environment. They need to be in an environment where they can do great work and be alongside people who they can learn from and share the passion for great work. Beyond that, they need to be doing great work, and ultimately what affects people the most is what they're doing on a day-to-day basis. It needs to be intriguing and engaging and people have to want to learn—and somewhere further down the list come things like compensation, stock options, and pay package.

Joe Kraus, Excite, Founder

How to Retain Top Employees

The key to retaining staff is to create a cohesive culture that builds loyalty and dedication to a larger purpose rather than simply how much money they can make.

People in Silicon Valley aren't comfortable talking about money, because the Valley has always been a place where people focused on building companies for a larger purpose. There's a great feeling in Silicon Valley that we're changing the way the world works, and stock options and employee ownership are all wonderfully empowering tools and they may bring rewards, but the ultimate goal is really about changing the world. That's one of the founding principles that motivates people in Silicon Valley. That's fundamentally why people aren't comfortable talking about money in Silicon Valley, because there is that history and it's usually rooted in doing something big and the financial rewards, if they come, come as a sort of wonderful gift that comes along with it, but are often not the beginning goal.

So when you build a culture and a mission that are about changing the world, changing the way companies do business, changing something big, that is generally one of the best ways to keep people focused and sort of culturally united.

That's the biggest way, but there are a lot of small things as well. Look at the way the workplace itself has changed. Look at Excite@Home. We ask people to put in a tremendous number of hours and work really hard, and in return we give back a lot: Bagel breakfasts every Monday morning, pizza lunches on Wednesday, a masseuse in-house, every sort of game you can imagine, slides in the building, dry cleaning, ice cream on Fridays, concierge services to help the staff do anything they need to get done. We are recognizing the fact that when we ask a ton of people to work tremendously hard, we need to bring them all the services that they may be missing outside of the workplace. This has fundamentally changed the relationship and the expectation of people who work here.

Kyle Shannon, Agency.com, Cofounder

The Biggest Challenges in Retaining Employees

Retaining people is certainly a huge challenge and there is a bit of a shift in the marketplace. The idea of company loyalty and being with a single company for 15 or 20 or 30 years is a dying philosophy. What it creates is a workforce in which employees are loyal to a company as long as they're personally engaged. If I have employees who are doing great work and they love what they're doing and they love their team, then they'll love the company and stick with the company. Three weeks later they might not be on that project. The phone might ring and somebody says, "Hey, do you want to come over here and try this out?" That puts the burden on the company to retain that person. We as a company can rely much less on traditional incentives like stock options and bonus programs. Those are almost table stakes these days. People expect that as part of the way of doing business. People that work for companies actually want more. They actually want to enjoy what they're doing. They want to be engaged, they want to be challenged, they want to be learning all the time, and they want to be doing great, exciting work. Those are not unreasonable requests. As human beings, people want to be doing things in their life that are adding to the world and that are adding to themselves. They're learning and growing.

What has changed is the power dynamic. It used to be that the corporation had all the power and set the rules. Employees played by them or didn't get to survive in the world. It's kind of a different world now and with information being power versus capital goods being power, the power has shifted to the employees. Employees sort of write their own checks. If a company has the attention of those employees, and has them engaged, and they feel that the company cares about them and is providing good work for them and a good environment for them, then they'll stay as long as that's the case. It's much more real time and much more fluid.

The disadvantage is that company loyalty is no longer a given. It's something that has to be earned over and over again. The advantage of it is if someone does leave, there's a good chance they might come back. They'll come back as long as they had a good enough experience while they were there and know that the environment is a supportive one. We've had a number of employees who have said, "I want to go try something different now." They do that and a year later they come back and start up again. We've had employees who have come back three or four times.

Companies need to accept the fact that that's the new environment. That's the new dynamic and it doesn't mean that companies shouldn't try to keep people. Companies still have to do all the right things, still have to have incentive programs, and still have to have great management that really takes care of their people.

Stephen Andriole, Safeguard Scientifics, CTO

Recruiting Must Be a Core Competency

The labor shortage is real and likely to get worse. In fact, finding talented professionals to staff product and service companies is emerging as perhaps the most important challenge facing companies in all stages of development. Companies that have identified employee recruitment and retention as core competencies are more likely to survive and grow than those that still recruit and retain the old-fashioned way. Creative solutions to this problem are no longer nice to have, but a necessity. Creative recruitment and retention strategies are no longer vitamin pills—they are painkillers.

The key to finding the right people is to see the right mix of technological prowess and management seniority to develop and deliver a successful product or service. Ideally, the management team has been there and done that, and is mature enough to deal with all varieties of unpredictable events and conditions. There are other ideal prerequisites: Experience in the target horizontal and/or vertical industry, the right channel connections, the ability to recruit and retain talented personnel, the ability to work industry analysts, communicate and sell. To this list we might all add a number of qualities, knowing full well that past success is not necessarily a predictor of future success.

John Ferber, Advertising.com, Cofounder

The Right Size Marketing Staff

We have a marketing staff of about 12 for a company of 300 people. We're probably light, meaning we should probably have another six to eight people. The strength of the marketing department is really based on how unique a company's product is, how much it's in demand, and whether the company is forced to proactively go out and generate business or business is just falling in its lap. So companies should try to hire marketers with great experience who can utilize that experience by coming to an organization. Hire intelligently and provide them all the support they need to execute effectively.

Mark DelVecchio, eWanted.com, VP Marketing

The Makings of a Marketing Team

One of the hardest things to do is to build a team, particularly when everybody else is trying to build one. It's a big challenge. I look at it in a couple of ways. First, I have a couple of really good online marketing professionals who have a number of years experience marketing major brands. My director of online marketing came from WB Online and French Digital Entertainment Network. So one push is I want to have some people who have been in this for a while.

The second push is, given that we're going to be embarking on a vertical marketing strategy, I'm trying to hire marketing entrepreneurs to head up my categories. Those people need to be a mixture of product marketers, brand managers, and category experts. It's not going to be as segmented as I've seen it elsewhere, where you have a product marketing person, a brand manager, and somebody who's a category specialist. I'm looking for people who are entrepreneurial who have those skill sets. They may be stronger in one area than another, but overall they're going to basically take these categories as businesses and run them as businesses for me.

It's also essential that the marketing department interacts with the business development department and the finance department for a company to be successful. Marketers need to be hand in glove with those departments, and also know the technology by working with the engineering department. It's fascinating to look back at my newspaper experience. The understanding that a reporter had about the pressroom or the circulation department was basically zero. One of my major goals, in all the companies I've worked for, is that people understand the whole business and not just their part of it. So working closely with business development and engineering and finance is absolutely essential to our success.

Joseph Howell, Emusic.com, CFO

Hire Risk-Takers

Tell employees interested in joining a startup that there's going to be a lot of risk here and a lot of uncertainty and a lot of change. Tell them, "We want you to participate with us in building this business and in the growth, but be aware that you didn't come to an environment because it was well established and stable. We're in the process of building something here."

It fundamentally takes a person who really accepts risk and enjoys taking risks. People who are looking for an opportunity to come to work in the same place with little change for a long period of time are probably going to be dissatisfied in this type of an environment.

The one constant we can offer is change. Hopefully that change is well-articulated and understood in the context of what we're doing and where we're going. But the fact of the matter is, it's change nonetheless, and change can be frightening and painful to a lot of people. Consequently, we have to determine from every employee we interview how comfortable they are with risk and with change. We find that there are many who are not comfortable with it or who think they might be but aren't sure. We need to focus our selection process on people who are both capable and willing to accept the change they're going to have to face here in this environment and put up with a lot of inconvenience sometimes.

Lynn Atchison, Hoovers, CFO

Know Your Prospective Employer

Number one, prospective employees should understand the product. They should ask, what is this company that I'm interviewing with doing in the marketplace? Does that make sense to me? Do I see that as a growth market?

Anyone who is interviewing in the near future needs to ask themselves, are they comfortable with the fact that this industry is probably going to consolidate? If an employee goes to work for an Internet company and that Internet company in six months gets bought by another company, then that may impact that person's career. However, she would have learned a lot and been exposed to an entirely different kind of economy.

Using Options as Compensation

The trend of options as a kind of currency used by companies will continue. What will happen is that the workforce will become more knowledgeable about options and they'll realize that the options are only valuable if the company grows and is successful. One of the things we see now from a recruiting standpoint is a real variation in how much people understand options.

Tim Bixby, LivePerson, CFO

The Importance of Money

Money tends to follow people. Make sure that every person the company hired is being maximized. Top executives need to force department managers almost on a daily basis to look at certain factors. Top executives need to push their managers to move people around and leverage all of their people resources.

What Prospective Employees Should Know About Internet Companies

It's more important than ever to understand what the company does, what they're selling, and that it's a real product. A prospective employee should even be able to get an idea about highly technical products. Akamai is a good example of this: It's essentially a bunch of clever Ph.D.s and they've come up with a great technology, but their concept is "we make the Web work faster." Everybody gets that. It makes complete sense. So even on the technical side you can evaluate the value that these companies are bringing pretty easily.

Louis Kanganis, Nerve.com, CFO

Rules for Joining an Internet Company

Prospective employees should look for smart, committed managers. A great idea without good management will fail. They should also look to see if there's been a lot of turnover, because it will give them a good idea of what to expect. Prospective employees must personally believe in the company and what it's doing. A large part of working at one of these companies is trying to get others (investors, business partners, employees, customers) excited about its vision and what the company is trying to accomplish. If an employee doesn't believe in those things, he won't be successful.

The True Value of Stock Options

As a prospective employee or business partner considering the value of stock options, the best formula is to work it backwards. The person should try to decide how much money he would need or be happy with for the opportunity in question and the related risk to be worth his effort. Then he should try to make a forecast of what he thinks the market value of the company could be worth in an appropriate market environment. Finally, he should see if his percent of the company, including hefty dilution, would get him to that number he needs to be happy.

When comparing the stock options packages of a public versus a private company, there really isn't much difference between the two. On the one hand there is greater liquidity in the public companies, and hence, a greater chance of actually exercising the stock for a profit. The private companies are riskier, since they need to get acquired or go public for investors or employees to profit, but the risk is generally more than offset by the much greater potential for appreciation in a private company's equity.

David Henkel, Agillion.com, CFO

Skills Needed at the Top

Good people at the top is the most important item to look for in Internet companies as a prospective employer. Good people should be able to attract other good people and money. It is also important that top management be able to work effectively together. Few companies today can be effectively run by a CEO who is a king or a dictator. The ability to benefit from the experience of the entire top management team is a plus.

The ability for companies to be nimble and adapt to change is also important. Today's competitor is tomorrow's acquisition and next week's free service. The landscape is constantly changing.

Keeping the Right People

The dynamic and fast changing nature of the Internet has attracted some of the country's best and brightest. The nature of this industry, however, is such that no one person can keep on top of everything that is happening. Accordingly, it is particularly important that employees work well with others. Not just "get along" with others, but be able to function effectively in teams. With rapid growth and competitive changes happening on an almost daily basis, teams of employees who can divide up responsibilities and trust each other to execute each person's part are very effective.

The Internet has a reputation as being dominated by very young employees. But as the industry moves more toward the mainstream, older and more experienced employees will find themselves increasingly in demand. As members of dynamic teams, experienced employees who are confident and self-assured will find their contributions of great value—even if they don't feel that they understand the industry very well.

Employees with solid functional experience in the many disciplines required by all businesses as they grow and become more complex will be in great demand by Internet companies as they grow. A willingness to work in management structures that are quite dynamic is also important. Finally, for businesses to grow rapidly there is often the need to just roll up your sleeves and do whatever needs to be done. An employee who is willing to try this dynamic environment and has at least some of these characteristics will probably do well.

It can be very exciting to work in this dynamic Internet environment. However, some personality types respond to this challenge by driving themselves to the point that they burn out. This is particularly true of people involved in projects. If a person has a skill that is critical to a project, and it is perceived that no one else on the project, or in the company, can perform this function, then the pressure to work long weeks can be tremendous. For some reason it seems that people subject to this problem are also poor at teaching others the skills they have.

Experienced project management should be able to detect this issue before it becomes critical. But it is also important for a company to "not put all of its eggs in one basket." The most immediate management response is to hire skilled personnel who have the ability to learn key skills from the employee facing possible burnout. Top management needs to continually identify areas where it faces such risks, and make sure that the necessary financial resources are devoted to resolving such problems.

Some companies offer special programs for extended time off after an employee has put in a certain number of years. But with the pace of activity in the Internet, it would be difficult to match such a program to the needs of the employees prone to burn out. The best solution is careful management attention to individual situations and a willingness to commit the necessary financial resources to actually solve the problem. As with many things in an environment of rapid growth, a flexible approach to deal with individual situations often works well.

Designing a Fair Compensation Package

When it comes to compensation for individual employees, both parties need to have some degree of flexibility. The basic tradeoffs that an early stage Internet company faces is how to attract the best key employees with the least cash and stock options. Employees coming from large companies can expect to have the entire bonus portion of their compensation replaced by stock-related compensation and the promise of a cash bonus in the future, when the company is on more solid financial ground. This may be acceptable to many people, but the difficulty is usually the toughest when the Internet company also proposes a reduced salary and limits upfront moving and other costs. Cash is at such a premium in the early stage of a company that any cash expenditure that can be avoided can be translated into a higher valuation on the next round of a staged funding.

The possibility of large rewards from future stock appreciation is the major financial "carrot" that Internet companies can hold out to employees. The value of this reward is difficult to determine, and, accordingly, most employees end up requiring a basic level of compensation on which they can live. What employees sometimes fail to take into account is that other income from a working spouse or investment returns from previous jobs may be sufficient to support a compensation structure that has a reduced salary and greater options. This is especially true of older employees who become risk averse. If employees would stand back and assess their entire financial picture, they would probably find that the lower level of salaries paid by Internet startup companies are easier to accept.

One item to consider is to request that the base salary be moved up to a level that is closer to the market level if the company is successful in raising additional funding. In this way employees can limit the amount of stock that they need to sell in order to cover living expenses.

Who Needs Middle Managers

Middle management does not gather a lot of press attention these days, but it is just as important as ever for businesses. One of the issues that Internet companies face is that there are so many challenges for top management to deal with, that there is less attention that can be devoted to the day-to-day running of the business. The opportunities for acquisitions and strategic partnerships are pervasive in the Internet space, and these opportunities often require the attention of top management due to their strategic nature.

Meanwhile, the day-to-day challenges of running the business are not any less. In fact, with the changing competitive and market environment, it is even more important than ever for management to be on top of the pricing, channel, and customer issues that are constantly in flux. This requires that a competent group of middle management personnel be developed if possible. The training and mentoring time of top management can be considerable in order to effectively develop and train such a group. However, the rewards can be significant. As long as the company maintains a flexible management structure that can respond quickly to changing conditions, this additional layer of management can be a significant benefit to a rapidly growing company. With many employees in Internet companies still being young and inexperienced in basic business fundamentals, the role of middle management can also be "adult supervision" for the creative and aggressive people who are attracted to Internet companies.

Alan Breitman, Register.com, CFO

Know the Financial and Business Fundamentals

Prospective employees need to look first and foremost at cash flow. A lot of companies are investing for the future and laying the foundation, but there should be some sort of contribution from the current business, as it exists today. Evaluate and assess whether this is viable in the long term. And if they are burning cash today, understand where the burn is coming from and when the inflection point happens. In other words, if a company's customer acquisition cost is supposed to trend down from $100 to $2, and is representing that that is going to happen over the next 12 months, it's possible to monitor that on a perspective basis to make sure the company is executing that plan.

The biggest problem in this recent Internet era is that a lot of companies had great ideas but were just not very far along on executing the plan or the strategy. Some of these companies would change strategy midstream, and that is a real warning sign. Either the first business model was not sound or the management didn't have the faith or the ability to execute on their original business plan so they shift gears midstream.

Also, financially, it's important to thumb through the financial statements, look at the footnotes, understand the capitalization of the company, and understand which investors have put their money in and believe in this company. Understand which banks have done deals and are willing to supply lines of credit to this company. Make sure that the company will be around in eight to 10 months. Most of these companies are burning cash.

Equally important is to look at profitability. When do companies think they're going to get profitable? What are the other competitors in the space doing? See what their growth trends and their life cycle look like, and see if the expectations that are out on the table match up. It's easy to get that kind of intelligence if a company is publicly traded, because there is published intelligence on the company and the business model and on how they perceive the space. It's much harder if it's not a publicly traded entity.

Also, be sure to know who the company's auditors are and who the company's attorneys are. Make sure they're "real" firms. Know the banking relationships that the company has, who the VCs are, who owns the company. Find out about turnover. Has there been a lot of turnover? Prospective employees should determine whether the position they're interviewing for was newly created or recently vacated. If it has been recently vacated, did someone move up within the organization or was somebody let go?

Be sure to understand stock options plans. Are they incentive or are they non-qualified options? What are some of the terms and conditions of the plan with respect to changing control? Learn whether the company is generating cash and when it projects it will generate cash if it's not. And financially, find out when management thinks the company is going to break even and start showing earnings.

Stock Up on Stocks

The advantages public companies garner from offering employees stock options are huge. Almost every employee has an ownership interest in this company, so everything that they do will help the company and potentially impact the stock price, impacting their own personal wealth. The amount of stock options that people get is not immaterial relative to their salaries. A customer service representative making $26,000 a year can have options that could be worth significantly more than what he would make in several years. That is the incentive.

For individuals evaluating the public versus the private stock option plans, the first thing to look at is whether the company has been taking a lot of non-cash compensation charges for issuing options that are way in the money; that could be potentially problematic. The other thing to look at is the stock option plan, the rights that are in there, and how and if it provides incentives for the employees the way it should. Someone can glean total stock options over total shares fully diluted or outstanding to see how big the portion of total options that are available for issuance can be diluted to the company. That's probably a good way of valuing it as well.

For us, it all starts at our stock and explaining to an employee that if he does his job as best he can, he can only help the stock price. To the extent that our stock goes up, he personally will be worth more, because the company will be worth more. From there we can tear down into how—depending on who I'm talking to and what group of the company—their direct efforts will help to impact the financial statements.

Joan Platt, CBS MarketWatch, CFO

The (Un)Changing Role of Stock Options

Stock options have always been a factor in compensation. I've been here for 20 years and stock options have always been key. Actually the difference is because the unemployment rate is so low. It used to be that a startup would offer options and could offer a lower salary. Today that's not true. Startups are offering the salary, bonus, and then the stock options on top of it.

If the company is privately held, the employees should get more shares. The risk is higher that it will never pop. For a while it didn't seem like there was any risk, as so many companies were going public. Now it's back as the market's much tighter.

An employee of a public company actually gets less stock, but is in an established public company, which should mean less risk. The evaluation is determining how successful the company will be in the long term and how interested the public investment community is in the company's market.

Options used to be a tool. And a better tool 10 to 20 years ago than it is today. Today it's a given. Today a company has to match everyone out there. Before, companies could use it or not; now people expect it, it's almost a guarantee.

Mary Dridi, WebMethods, CFO

The Financial Side of Hiring

Options are an excellent recruiting tool and are an excellent thing for companies in general. If the prospective employer puts the proper emphasis on them, and makes people understand not only what options are worth to them but how they can really impact the value of those options, they can be a great tool.

We like the fact that all employees are owners. We want to really give them the sense of responsibility and ownership and how they can affect that not only for themselves but for other shareholders. That's very important. Options won't go away. It's possible they will become an even more meaningful part of compensation plans; we see people becoming more and more appreciative of options.

Candidates, however, have difficulties comparing options offered by two or more companies. I've had many, many conversations where people say, "But Company X offered me 10,000 and you're only offering me 5,000"—and all they are looking at is the absolute number of shares. Then I would ask a couple of simple questions. How many shares do they have outstanding? What are their revenues? How do you compare their potential opportunity to ours? Who is backing the company? And their response would be they don't know. So I would try to explain that it's like comparing how many yen you're going to get versus how many dollars and only looking at the absolute number and not the underlying value. You can't do that type of comparison.

Employers should never do a reverse stock split on employees—and candidates should look out for this. Although the real value has not changed, perceptually it's a negative thing in the employees' minds. Employees who were given a huge amount of options later find out that it was just because the base of the shares was so large. So they thought they were getting a lot more than they were—especially if they only looked at the number of options without regards to the number of shares outstanding.

So everyone has to be careful. Employees don't need to go through a lot of mathematical calculations, but when they are comparing one company's option grant to another they may want to look at the number of shares outstanding and take that into consideration, especially when the size of the option grants are significantly different. Prospective employees also may want to take into consideration what funding stage the company is in. If it's an earlier stage company, they're most likely going to do many more rounds of financing versus a company that may be very close to an IPO; the number of shares being offered will be higher and the exercise price will be lower in an earlier stage company.

Asking the profitability question, and asking when and if the company plans to go public can also be beneficial. Most of those answers will be vague for obvious reasons. It's probably more important to look at who the financial backers are, what kind of companies they have backed, how much money has been invested to date and how much the company actually has in the bank today. It is also important to get an understanding of the market opportunity the company addresses.

It would be interesting to know what the revenues are, assuming the company is producing revenues. A private company may not share much financial information with a prospective employee. So prospects who aren't able to get detailed financial information should look at the number and quality of customers and how the customer base has increased. It's going to be even harder to get information on projections, but if the prospective employer will give the employee an idea of when it expects to reach profitability, that would be helpful to know. What's important is looking at the backers, and just talking to the employees. A prospective employee can get a good idea about the company from seeing the confidence of the employee base, getting an understanding of who the management team is, and feeling how comfortable and confident he is with that management team.

My decision to join WebMethods at a very early stage was based on three things: My confidence in management's ability to execute, my belief in the market opportunity, and the fact that a well-respected firm, FBR Technology Venture partners, had backed the company.

Having said all that, it really comes down more to which company and management team does the prospective employee believe in and think has the greater potential. So the real decision should be based on confidence and belief in the company and the management team.

In our case, we tried very hard throughout the entire IPO process to not make the IPO too big of a deal or the end game. We pretty much said this is not the finale, this is actually the beginning of a new phase in the company's life.

We had an IPO party and that type of thing, but there wasn't a huge amount of celebration, because we continued to tell people that they have to focus, they have to execute. Execution is even more important now than ever before.

A year before the IPO we only had about 70 employees, and by the time of the IPO we had more than 250. So the majority of employees were relatively new to the company, and everybody had options, so they knew that it wasn't about the short term but about the long-term value. Because of the market volatility and other things, it is important that employees not focus on the day-to-day changes in the stock price—we emphasize that we can't do much about the short-term volatility in the stock market. What we can influence, however, is the long-term value of the stock based on our performance and our execution. We have a lot more control over that in the long term.

With respect to attracting employees, it certainly can be easier to hire employees after the company has filed its S-1 and during the IPO process. We attracted quite a few during that time period; companies should take advantage of that window. We looked at what we were going to need over the next couple of months and moved forward for those hires, and knew we could do that from a cost standpoint. It's obviously beneficial to the employees and to the company.

Sometimes, before an IPO, a company is attracting different types of people. When a company is in an earlier stage it will attract the people who are more entrepreneurial, the ones willing to take more risks. After the IPO that changes. It's not that after the IPO a company won't get people who are very entrepreneurial or willing to take risks. It's just that over time, the firm will attract a different type of person. There are a lot of people who would prefer to start at the company after it has gone public. That just gives them a little bit more security.

John Somorjai, Keen.com, VP Business Development

How to Establish Goals

We establish goals for our group every six months. We have written performance reviews and we evaluate everyone on what their goals were the prior six months and how they performed against those goals. Then we set new goals going out for the next six months.

The goals are primarily on the two metrics that we follow: registration and revenue. The goals that we set in business development and the performance review process are membership and revenue goals and we focus on certain categories. For example, we have people who are responsible for the computer category and others who are responsible for the health category. We set goals for each category.

Todd Love, yesmail.com, Senior VP Business Development

Measuring Success

From a management standpoint I'm a big fan of quarterly performance reviews. That way there are no surprises, and also wounds haven't progressed so much that they can't be repaired. So we all work together on a quarterly basis, and I have a pretty lean and mean machine established to be able to do so without spending months at a time reviewing people.

As far as success is concerned, it's really a combination of a lot of things, some objective and some subjective. The objective parts have to do with how many partners an employee has brought on, how many names he has contributed to the database, and how he has contributed to the database growth. Beyond that, in any given quarter we'll look at the previous quarters to see what the aggregate response rate is of those consumers that an employee has brought into the database. We have a team of people who do nothing but pre-qualify sites and prospects to go after, so we ask our employees how many of these pre-qualified folks have they closed? Are they going after what we think they need to go after?

And of course, as we're learning our metrics these things are changing pretty regularly. And as we're learning seasonal issues, these goals will change on a quarterly basis. That's another reason why every three months is a good time to sit down with these folks again.

It's really a combination of quantity and quality. Management has to get employees focusing on quantities to some respect, because their probability of closing quality will increase. But measurement of quality usually is three to six months hindsight.

Also, the A is for effort. Is the employee in the office a lot? Business development is one area in which if someone is in the office he's probably doing something wrong.

We have the team split up among an East Coast director, a Midwest director and a West Coast director. They have R&D and administrative support beneath them. So we have the hunter-and-gatherer approach in each of the regions. Then we have a strategy-and-implementation person. Somebody who's kicking the tires of technology, kicking the tires of new businesses that we think we want to get into at any given time, and somebody who's going to help with the integration of new initiatives. An example of this is that we're getting into the loyalty business. The points business, so to speak. So we've partnered with CMGI and Net Incentives and Alta Vista to create a loyalty solution for the CMGI companies. Not only are we putting new requirements in different parts of our own company, but we have to help expedite this for the other companies involved as well. So we need a full-time person to roll out these things as we get into them.

Then each business development person on each coast also has a side initiative that they're responsible for. We're growing our B2B database by leaps and bounds. We have somebody looking over that as well as someone in the international and wireless spaces. Then, once those initiatives get fully baked out, strategy and implementation takes them over and rolls them out.

Chris Dobbrow, Real Names, Senior VP Business Development & Sales

How to Build a Business Development Team

In order to build a business development team, the hiring manager has to have a good understanding of the vision and the key goals of the organization. Then it's the product: Is there a strong product element to business development, deals that the business development team is going to be doing, or is it really more marketing and sales type relationships? I'm very much a structure-oriented individual, where if we understand our vision and mission more and what our goals are in the organization, it makes it far easier to build a team around those strategies.

A strong product technical focus to the position would clearly shape the type of person who a manager would hire as well as how she might organize her team. If it's marketing and sales related then the manager can look for those kinds of people and organize the team around what the key initiatives are. So it's kind of an open book.

Sometimes it's a combination of all of those things, which is really what we are: We're everything from a brand management platform to an enabling infrastructure technology. It requires a different skill set for different people doing different types of business development deals. Ultimately a business development team should be a mix of people with different skills. A team shouldn't comprise people who are clones of each other, a team should be diverse, because that diversity helps build a great learning and motivational environment for everyone on the team. I try to strive for people who are really passionate and who want to learn more. They don't have to know everything, but they want to learn more and they have a willingness to do that. They have analytical minds and the creativity to look at the blank canvas and see what it might look like.

Daniel Conde, Imandi.com, Director of Business Development

Diverse Skills Sets Make a Team

The term business development is sort of vague. It can mean a lot of different things. So managers need to look at the characteristics of what kind of skill sets they need for good business development, then find people who have worked in business development. But people with experience at different yet relevant jobs are good, too. For example, because there is salesmanship involved, people who have customer and sales experience would be good, because they have sold externally. They understand contracts, negotiations, and deal terms. The candidate need not have been in a regular sales position, though. It could be someone who has done OEM deals and other deals like that. But it shouldn't be somebody who is into only the hard-sell aspects. The prospective employee has to understand analysis to quantify the deals. That could either be the same person who has a sales side and an analytical side, or could be two people: one to do analysis and one to do the sales. Ideally, however, managers should hire people who can do both sides, because it's inefficient and time consuming for somebody to just talk to another person or partner and then come back and ask somebody else to do an analysis. It's also good to have one person who understands the whole deal.

On the other hand, if a company deals with different vertical industries, then it needs somebody with industry experience. If a firm is dealing with media companies, then maybe it needs somebody with experience in knowing how to quantify different types of media deals or placement in other firms. And if it's a technology business development team, then the company needs somebody with a technology background as well.

It's hard to generalize how to build a business development team, but managers should look at what are the main points that drive a new deal, whether it's technology, contract terms, or getting exposure to the right types of people at the partner firms. Just like in traditional sales, business development teams need people who have access to high-level managers who can make wide-ranging business decisions. Therefore, having people with the right kind of high-level contacts helps as well.

In an ideal world managers should build a team that has people with different skill sets. In the *Seven Samurai*, or its Western remake, *Magnificent Seven*, there were swordsmen or seven gunslingers who were all different characters. But they were pretty good generalists in many ways so they could help each other out in a clutch. So it's possible to look at it that way, too: Don't have too many super-specialists who cannot pitch in to help each other.

In a tight job market it's often hard to build the ideal team quickly, so find out who is available and then build the right kind of team around them. And be pragmatic. A manager waiting for that perfect team of seven samurai may not get that for a long time, because it's a tight job market. Build a team around the available and trustworthy people.

Bernie Dietz, WebCT, VP Business Development

Use Your Contact Network

I was successful building a business development department of 16 people in a short time by relying heavily on personal references from the people already in the department and in the rest of the company. The benefit that business development has in recruiting is that it is a job that requires a lot of networking and interaction among other business development professionals. I often come across people who are talented and would make great additions to my team. By building relationships this way it's possible to better see the potential of someone to fit into the culture of the group and the company overall. I also network with other business development VP's, trading résumés of potential additions when I don't have a slot to fill with others who do.

Mark Bryant, LifeMinders.com, VP Business Development

Have the Right Hiring Process

Building a business development team starts in the hiring process. It's important to hire the most talented, committed, driven people possible regardless of whether they've had experience in this industry. Many times people make the mistake of hiring someone because they worked at Yahoo!, and that doesn't necessarily make them a good candidate for business development success.

It's all in the fundamentals. Does this person have a track record of exceeding objectives, is she comfortable in an environment that changes on the fly, is she comfortable when we negotiate an agreement on Monday and then have to renegotiate that agreement on Wednesday? People need to be comfortable in an environment where the objectives change.

Robin Phelps, DigitalOwl.com, VP Business Development & Cofounder

Build a Team Whose Members Have Diverse Skills

It is important to find and hire people for the business development role who have a balance between sales, business, and technical skills. It helps if they have prior experience that shows the ability to recognize and close sales deals that were forward thinking or firsts in their company and that resulted in long-term business.

Strong business development people are usually big-picture thinkers and tend not to be detailed people. Therefore, a good business development team will include at least one person to support the team by specifying, following up on, and completing the details.

Over the next couple of years business development staff will begin to be an initial hire at startup companies, and it will be a key part of the executive management at most companies. Business development teams will also have engineering/operations responsibility in order to support more complex and longer-lasting partner agreements.

Andrew Wolfe, SONICblue, CTO

The Makings of a CTO

Obviously the role of the CTO is different at every company, but at S3 my primary responsibility is to help set the strategic direction of the company as a whole and to develop and maintain relationships with various kinds of technology partners who will help us to build better products in the future. Also, I work with the various product groups in terms of product planning. I help them determine how to bring new features and new capabilities to our various products and how to get our products to work together in more interesting ways, so that we can devise more of a total solution than a group of individual products.

The biggest difference in the role of CTO at S3 versus others is that this is a product company. For a lot of Internet companies a CTO is somewhat of an information systems manager, where they set up the infrastructure to provide information services. They design the architecture of server farms and software systems and whatnot. S3 is not an information services company, it's a product company. It's more like a consumer electronics company. So my role is not in information systems, but rather in helping our divisions design products that our customers will later use to connect to various information systems.

But to be successful in either type of company a CTO needs to have a broad knowledge of the industry to be able to understand new technologies quickly, because they change every day. It's also important to be able to develop and maintain relationships with a wide variety of other kinds of partners in the industry. Being a CTO is primarily a listening job: listening to what's going on at other companies, listening to what's going on with competitors, listening to what's going on in startups that are developing new markets and new product categories, and listening to customers and understanding what kind of problems they're trying to solve and what kind of new technologies they want to see in the future. CTOs are taking all that knowledge, all those things they can go out and glean from other people, condensing it, filtering it, and spreading that knowledge throughout the company so that employees can develop products that address a lot of these outside concerns.

The CTO can also expect to interact with the CEO. Our CEO calls me about every 20 minutes and I go to his office. This is the only place I've ever been a CTO, but here it's a very, very close relationship. We talk several times a day. He confers with me on a wide range of strategic issues. I consult him every time there's a decision that needs to be made that really effects the direction of the company. Basically, he has sent me on a mission to go out and find opportunities for the company to get into new areas, new technologies, and new relationships. Then I go out and find those opportunities and filter them. We see maybe 300 to 400 opportunities a year to work with other companies. I assess them, make recommendations, and then take them back to him, where he essentially makes the final call as to where the dollars go.

Building a Solid Technology Team

The most important thing to look for when building a technology team is smart people. There's no question about it. A few very smart, creative people go a long way in terms of making a company successful. There's nothing that can make up for that.

The other thing the company needs is a vision. It needs a bunch of people who can work together who know specifically how they want to somehow change the world in the next year or two or a bit longer depending on the industry. But for the types of things we're doing that are Internet or network-product related, our time frame is a year or two. We are always asking, "How do we change what people do? How do we change how they do it?" And if a manager can get a group of people all thinking on the same page in terms of accomplishing something great and something new, he'll have a good team. In our case the big idea lately has been to change the way people listen to music. That's been our big push with the RIO product line.

If a company can get a group of smart, preferably experienced people to start thinking about how that company can change the way that consumers do something, they quickly start to generate new ideas and new solutions, and then it's easy to get a lot of other people excited about working with them to deliver a product.

To find these people, a hiring manager should go find other successful companies and try to convince their employees that his company's product are more interesting so they will come work for his firm.

In terms of management resources, experience is key. In most cases just try to go find experienced industry veterans and attract them by being in a more exciting product area. In some cases we've also found people within our own company with engineering jobs who seem to have the skills to do this well, who have been through several projects and are ready to simply move to a different role. So we've done that as well.

Technical skills are very much in demand. Skilled marketing people are always in demand. In the end a lot of this business is about finding out what people want, finding out what people will pay for, and defining it correctly the first time. These are all very schedule-driven businesses. Companies have to get things right. Having marketing teams that can go out and understand consumer needs and then position the firm's product to solve those consumer needs is critical as cycles get shorter.

The other thing that's difficult is program management. We tend to focus heavily on the creative part of the engineering—the guys who sit down and write the software for a new feature, or who design the user interface, or who design the circuits for a new product. That's all critical; we couldn't operate without that. But there's another piece that really defines successful companies, and that is the ability to do things right the first time, the ability to do things on time, on budget; the program management skills, the people who can manage projects, keep them on schedule, understand the technology, understand the risks and manage those risks are critical, and they are very, very difficult to find.

Neil Webber, Vignette, Cofounder & CTO

The Role of the CTO

The most important role of the CTO is acting as the translator between the executive level management of the company and the technology aspects of the company. The role is bi-directional. It's being able to translate in both directions from the executive to the technical guy. It's also a matter of translating the technical guys who may be coming up with some neat stuff but don't understand how to position it or how it fits into the company strategy. That's sort of the day-to-day role of the CTO.

Here's kind of an absurd example to illustrate the point: If the marketing department says, "Gee, if only we could make a Star Trek transporter, imagine how much money we could make. Here's all the people who would want it, here's how much they can pay for it, yada, yada, yada." Obviously it's not possible to build a Star Trek transporter, but it's possible to get the entire company excited about the possibilities of, "Gee, imagine what we could do with this thing." Your role as CTO is to say, "Well, we can't build a

Star Trek transporter, but here's the thing we can build." The CTO should understand how that would meet the requirements of what the company was trying to do.

A CTO should also focus on the high-level strategic technology developments and how a company needs to be positioned for that. A lot of CTOs don't operate on that high level; they're much more comfortable playing the role of chief architect. They're down there with the technical guys helping them design a database scheme, or breaking up the systems into modules, or doing what would basically be senior architect level type things. And there's certainly a need for that in a company, but that's not the role of the CTO in a software product company. The CTO needs to be operating on a much higher level and let the guys who are in the system on a day-to-day basis do that other kind of work.

The Basis for Building a Technology Team

Building a technology team goes in phases in a company's growth. In the early days we actually focused a lot more on just hiring intelligent, competent, experienced engineers. We didn't try to look for people with specific experiences in specific areas because, at a startup company, everything changes all the time.

If I looked for a developer who had a specific expertise, it could very well be that three months later I didn't need that expertise anymore, and hopefully if I hired him there would be something else that he would be good at. So we always looked at just general maturity and ability to deal with a startup environment.

In the early days we tended to hire much more experienced guys than a lot of startups do. Often people look for the kids right out of school who will work 24 hours a day. I preferred to hire people who had been in the industry for a while and who had the experience and who could deal with all of the changes that we were going to go through as a startup.

Dwight Gibbs, The Motley Fool, Chief Techie Geek

How the CTO Fits Within a Highly Technical Organization

The Motley Fool grew very organically. In the old days, once my stress level got to a certain point, I would hire another techie to help me out. I assigned our Web site operations to the first guy I hired so I could concentrate on our AOL site. At that point almost all of our business was on AOL. That's where the revenue was, so that was where I focused my attention. Eventually, I couldn't keep up with the internal tech operations—user support, networking, PBX support, etc.—so we hired another techie to take that over. Essentially, we hired techies to address wherever we were bleeding the most. Finally, after we got to about 15 people, I realized that this growth strategy was somewhat less than optimal. We needed some organization and a growth plan. With that in mind, we separated the TechDome into functional groups, appointed team leads, and put together a rational growth plan. As we've grown we've had to reorganize a couple of times within the TechDome.

The Motley Fool has a fairly unique, non-traditional work environment. That is reflected in the titles and names of our tech teams. My title is Chief Techie Geek. The seven tech groups are DORC (Developmentally Oriented Research Crew), which is the tech R&D group and is modeled after Xerox's PARC (Palo Alto Research Center); Inter-Galactic Lords of Doom (a.k.a. InterGLOD, a.k.a. IGLOD), which handle desktop support, server support, network engineering, security, etc. and in most companies would be called MIS; the DEAD, or Database Engineering Analysis and Design group, which handles all things database; WebDev, the Web development group; AppDev, the application development group; Fifth Elephant, which handles quality assurance and technical documentation; TechTrain, which is the technical training group and offers classes for Outlook, Excel, Work, PowerPoint, Access, HTML, Project, several internal apps and anything else for which we need training. As you can see, I gave my folks a lot of latitude in naming their groups.

My role within these groups encompasses many areas. I'm basically where the technology buck stops. One area of focus is technical strategy. I'm the one who translates company goals to technology goals and guides the determination of the technical strategies to support those goals. Part of my job is to communicate the company goals to the TechDome and show how our tech goals support the company goals. I have seven managers with whom I work very closely. They are responsible for translating tech goals to the group and then to individual goals. But I am responsible for keeping the TechDome aligned with the rest of the company.

I also spend a significant amount of time working on vendor relations. This is because we don't really have vendors. We have partners. We're not like some large companies who send out RFQs (requests for quotes) for everything they buy and go with the lowest price. We try to find companies that we can really work with and get them to customize their solutions for us. Some examples are Akamai, Cisco, Compaq, and Microsoft. We've worked with all these companies very closely and then they've been very helpful in solving our problems. I spend a lot of time growing those relationships.

The rest of my time is spent on project management and that elusive thing called management. The details of management are hard to describe but they are critical. Management deals a lot with employee development and individual alignment. Day to day it means I send and receive lots of email, talk on the phone, and go to lots of meetings.

When I started, I was doing all of the hands-on tech work—database administration, programming, networking, hardware/software support. Happily for the past two years I haven't written one line of code. In fact, when the last bit of my code was removed from production, there was much rejoicing all around. While I haven't been doing the hands-on work, I've maintained my knowledge of what's going on, what we're doing, and what's possible. I have become fairly adept at determining how technology can support the business and ensuring that we have the technical resources we need to address the business needs that we have now and those that we will have in the future.

One of my areas of expertise is that management thing. Through management I make sure that the TechDome addresses the needs of both our internal customers (the people within Fool headquarters) and our external customers (those on our Web site). I try to get my folks to manage customer expectations. If you manage people's expectations, no one gets upset. They know what to expect and are not surprised. That applies to both internal and external customers. Internally we need to deliver projects when we promise to and make sure that they are to spec. Externally, if we are doing maintenance on our site, we need to tell our customers well in advance that certain parts of the site will be inaccessible. I have to do this within the TechDome: "These are the projects we will be expected to deliver"; "These are the tools and languages you can expect to use"; "I expect you to put in X hours a week"; "This is the kind of compensation you can expect." It all comes down to making sure that everyone is on the same page. It sounds incredibly simple, but it's not.

I also interact heavily with the rest of the management team. We have a CEO who is ultimately responsible for the business, but we have something called an executive committee that basically provides information for the decisions, sets the priorities, ensures execution and that kind of thing. I sit on the executive committee, as do our two founders, Tom and David Gardner, our CEO, our CFO, our chief legal officer, our COO, and several other top-level managers. We determine what's strategically important to the Fool and set the company goals. I inform the committee from a technology standpoint. I am also the tech liaison to the other departments in the Fool. Once the executive committee sets the company goals, it's my responsibility to take them down to the tech level and determine what we need to do to support those goals. It's that alignment thing.

How to Foster Creativity in a Large Tech Team

It's pretty simple to foster creativity in TechDome. We have to hire excellent technical managers and delegate responsibility to them. Keep in mind that technical managers aren't the same as regular managers. Obviously, technical managers have to be good managers. They also have to understand the technology. If they don't, their staff will not respect them. Techies can sense incompetent poseurs and good techies will not tolerate them. So if someone is trying to pose, he is just going to get slammed. And it is likely to be exceptionally brutal. So when I'm in meetings with some of my staff and we're discussing different technical solutions, I'll often say, "Clearly I'm not the best person to make a decision on what the best technology is. That's why you're here." And that is the truth. I've hired very smart people, so it's up to them to say what they think is the best technology or best approach. I'm more concerned with the business end. I'm the one asking, "Does this make good business sense for the Fool?" For this reason, we don't always do exactly what we want to. It has to be balanced with the company's needs. If we did everything we wanted to do just from a technology perspective, we'd take all the money the Fool has and then some, and spend it all on tech. But a company can't do that and be sustainable. It's my job to make sure that we balance the business needs with the technology needs.

The best way to foster creativity is to give people as much latitude as possible and encourage bold thinking. We also have a pretty liberating environment that encourages collaborative thinking. We don't have offices. We don't have rigid policies: no set business hours, no set vacation time, no set sick leave, no dress code. We also have a well-stocked game room. In short, we treat our employees like adults and expect them to act like adults. They generally do. This relaxed environment attracts creative techies and stimulates their creative juices.

In the technology industry right now people are the resources most in demand. Technology in and of itself is worthless. It's how you use it. The funny thing is that right now the industry is not hurting for the traditional tech skill: programming and system administration. It's dying for project management skills and really good quality assurance and testing skills. Project management is just a tremendous need because techies who can code are relatively easy to find. Finding someone who can manage a large project is a different story.

Our software has advanced to the point where it's not a case of one guy or one gal handling a single project. We have multiple techies on each project, and so someone who actually understands technology and project management and can execute and motivate is tremendously valuable and in short supply.

Another tough skill set to find is quality assurance (QA) testers. It has been in high demand because most techies approach applications thinking like a techie and not like a user. What we value in our QA folks is their ability to think like average Joe user, but find problems and are able to diagnose why they are happening.

What it Takes to Become a Leader

There are two basic traits that help people develop into leaders at any position within a company. The first is innovation. Good leaders will try new ideas and search relentlessly for better solutions. The second is honesty. Leaders have to paint a true and realistic picture of the way things are and bring uncompromising honesty to all of the things they touch, great and small. These are two of The Motley Fool's core values.

Peter Stern, Datek, CTO

Finding Top Tech Staffers Who Fit the Team

Companies like ours are limited mostly by their ability to enable business ideas, or resolve business problems, or make business solutions out of technology. There are not that many people who do the basic analyst's job of understanding the technology, understanding what the customer needs, and being able to tell the programmers how to build it, and that's still the limiting factor for a lot of companies, including ours.

There are a lot of smart people, great people, but the small number of people who at a high level can determine good business versus technology tradeoffs is still kind of limiting us. That's an experience problem, and the population of people who have those skills or experience at using those skills are needed by the industry a lot. Not Web producers or programmers—it's always hard to find good people in anything—but those people who have that *je ne sais quoi*, knowing how to build good stuff, without the clue factor, those people are pretty rare.

Anyone who has desire can learn any technical skill; it might take them a year, it might take them six months, if they've learned these kinds of skills before it might take them a few weeks. I am not so concerned that they already have years experience with Java, I am not so concerned that they have years of experience designing Web sites, I am concerned that when they look at a product or look at a service they see what it does and what it could do and understand how to build the thing the way it should be.

Take a person who can look at a cell phone and say, "You know what, if I designed this cell phone, I would rearrange the buttons, because I use this button a lot more than I use the other buttons, so that button should be where my thumb is." That kind of person should be able to apply the exact same talent to good Web page layouts, or determining which features on a product do not make any sense, or that the underlying architecture of a product does not match what it is supposed to do. They can do that whether they are talking about their cell phone or talking about Java code or talking about a Web site.

Our technology team is involved in every aspect of the company, and it is frustrating sometimes because there are only so many technical resources we can throw at any given project. Sometimes company executives feel that the technology team is a limiting factor and they should go elsewhere to get something done or build a product that doesn't involve technology, but of course that doesn't really exist anymore in our business. My technical teams are involved in all aspects of the company and a lot of areas of the company cannot proceed with evolving their business or making it more efficient at attracting new customers or building new products without resources from the techno-crews.

Warwick Ford, Verisign, CTO

Interacting With the CEO

I am in an interesting position. My strategic technologies unit is separate from the engineering organization where mainstream development is done. I interact directly with the corporate executives, the engineering organization, and the marketing and sales organizations. Getting all these groups on the same page where technology is concerned is really key to my job. I interact directly with our CEO, Stratton Sclavos, a great deal. Stratton has a strong technological background and is very much a part of shaping the technology vision along with other aspects of the corporate vision.

How Reputation Attracts Stars

In my case, which may well be different from those of other CTOs, I am directly responsible for just a small specialized technology strategy team. The approach is to keep it lean and mean, and I've been fortunate to find some exceptionally talented individuals who have all the skills needed to fulfill this role. While there is enormous competition for talent today, VeriSign has fared better than many other companies, through building a reputation as one of the best employers in the Internet game.

Ron Moritz, Symantec, CTO

Balancing New Staff With Veterans

Meshing new hires with veteran staffers is an interesting challenge for a CTO. I'm an old engineer at heart; I still have passion for the creation and innovation and I really like to get into the details when I can. Ultimately, the CTO's role is much broader. It's not just about innovation here. I have a number of sustaining technologies, what I call infrastructure technologies, that my groups are responsible for. The challenge is to find the balance between new engineers coming into Symantec (by new I don't necessarily mean lacking in experience, I simply mean outsiders), and a very deep and experienced team that has been around for many, many years at Symantec.

There are people here who are very senior, key individuals with nine, 10, 11 years tenure, unprecedented in this industry. These people have gained a certain expertise that we don't want to lose, but we need to bring in more people to grow the business and to focus our efforts. Good engineers are very hard to find in the industry. Consequently, the need to maintain a comfort zone for your existing teams is important, so they don't feel that they're being moved aside. Managers have to bring in the new people to energize the company in a direction that it hasn't gone before. A clear example is Symantec, a company built on a foundation of Windows that is interested in the enterprise market. In this market it is the Unix operating system (I'm using a generic terminology to cover the gambit of Solaris, Linux and others), that is important. As the company shifts from the consumer and the retail box space to an enterprise focus, its core engineering capability also changes. That makes the older engineers, whose experience is rooted somewhere else, a little uncomfortable.

So, the challenge I have is finding the balance between the skills of the existing employees and the skills needed from the outside to move the company forward. I can highlight some of those skills today. The fact is, there is a shortage of engineers these days. And when a company is fortunate enough to get them, they are finicky. It's almost like working with artists. If a manager can gather enough momentum and herd them in the same direction, then they're a powerful bunch. But because they're like artists, each one has individual ideas, each one has their own thoughts, and in many ways they're all over the place. It's hard to keep them focused, happy, and energized. Keeping their collective eyes on the same goal is a significant challenge from a management perspective.

Dermot McCormack, Flooz.com, CTO & Cofounder

Who Is in Demand

It's really across the board. If a company has a good Oracle DBA on staff, they should hold onto him. Also, finding great network engineers, people who really understand networking, is probably one of the harder things to do. This role will only become more important as the networks get bigger and the traffic on these networks gets greater.

The availability of good Java programmers should increase over the next few years, but they are still a scarce and expensive resource. Another trend is a demand for technologists and programmers who have experience with both newer technologies and legacy systems. They understand what a mature system looks like and are familiar with the tools to build a new system. Candidates with this skill set will become extremely valuable.

Pavan Nigam, Healtheon, Cofounder

Balancing Two Disparate CTO Roles

There are two hats I wear and therefore two organizations that I manage. One hat is a pure CTO hat, and for that I have a CTO architecture council that has our senior brains in it. Within WebMD we have a hierarchy of fellows and chief engineers and principal engineers. In a company of about 7,000 we cumulatively have less than a dozen of them, so you can imagine what a brain trust that is. That is what I call the CTO architecture council, and that is the group I'm looking to in terms of staying on top of all the latest technology developments.

The other hat I wear is in my role as executive vice president of all our product divisions, all our Internet product divisions—I have five of them. The five divisions all have general managers who hold responsibility. One is a consumer division that is focused on Internet consumer services; the second is a provider division that is focused on the services we provide to doctors; the third is an employer division, which handles services we provide to employer Internet services; the fourth division is what we call the platform services, and it is all the core underlying technologies we develop for supporting these and user services; and the fifth division is more the network operation side of it, managing the operation side of all these different services. All five divisions are reporting to me as executive vice president of all the product services. The overall size of the team is somewhere between 1,500 and 2,000, so it's fairly large.

Managing is easy for me, because I have strong general managers for all these five divisions. They have to be held responsible, so they go ahead and do what's needed. The challenge WebMD has is to keep track of the latest technology and services, and to make sure that we are exploiting facilities between the various services and technologies. That's where the CTO architecture council makes recommendations about how we should be using wireless technologies in a consistent way across everything we do at WebMD, or that we should be declaring XML as a standard for everything across what's going on, etc. We don't want every division to have its own technology strategy, so we've created this thing on the side with some of the best brains. These brains also belong to the various divisions, so we keep it very non-threatening in nature.

That's how I manage it: have good general managers and have some of the smartest technology brains and make them all stay marching in the same direction.

Integrating Technologies From Acquisitions

Integrating different technologies and different technology departments into one central core is not easy, but we do two things. First, for some of the fundamental technologies, like what platform the portal is going to run on, we make the decision right away and we use the mission critical platform that Healtheon developed right in the beginning as the fundamental platform for everything. When we acquire a new company that goes with the territory. We have to go ahead and use the one platform as the delivery platform for all the services. So we don't spend time arguing every time we make an acquisition.

The second thing, however, is that we believe in staging different technologies, so just because we've acquired a company, we don't require the company to go and transform everything to some new set of technologies. If what they have works fine, then we integrate that into our system and we evolve. Then we can take a look at what makes sense and what doesn't make sense, do the portal, do the core platform technologies, etc. Many times we don't have to go and make anything, we can treat one of our acquisitions like a third-party service or a third-party technology base—all we do is integrate into our portal. Let's take Yahoo! as an example: The core platform is whatever Yahoo! has, but it also has so many services and virtually every service Yahoo! has is delivered by third parties.

In our case the core technology for our consumer portal is one singular WebMD technology. How do we do a single sign-on, how is security managed, how is personalization managed, how is navigation managed? Everything is done in one and only one way. But the actual delivery of the service—which might be entering a lab order or entering a pharmacy order—can be carried out by different technologies. If it works, then in the beginning we just integrate it like any third-party service and we punt on the decision as to what level of technology conversion we want to do. It becomes more of a business decision about what is going to cost us more.

So this is how we can do it. When I explain this to Wall Street I just say that we're pragmatic about it. The core portal will have to be one and only one, and has to be an experience we're not going to compromise on; but the delivery of the actual services at the back end, whether on a Solaris platform or a Microsoft platform or whatever, is something where we'll make a change when and if it makes sense.

Michael Wolfe, Kana Communications, VP Engineering

Breadth of Knowledge Versus Depth of Knowledge

Individuals starting in technology fields have to strike a balance between depth and breadth. When you're in an academic environment depth is rewarded. It's easy to graduate from college with deep technical knowledge, but not really have much of an idea how those things translate into real world problems. Unless a person wants to go into teaching or research, which not many people do, he needs to start finding business problems that need solving. It's almost like a doctor who knows how to do an operation, but doesn't know why smoking is a bad idea. High-tech employees need to know the larger context with which they are working. To make technology their career, individuals need to go deep into some of the fundamentals, but they also need to keep up with the trade press, network, and go to different companies and understand how they position their technology. They need to look more at how people are using technology to execute their business strategy. It's breadth over depth in general. The more senior somebody gets the more they need to focus on breadth. Early on it's OK to be a little more deep.

My knowledge is very much around software and computer science. I am not a hardware person, I'm not a biotech person, I'm not a networking person. So I see a lot of the opportunities in software, especially for someone just getting started in technology. Software drives all of these devices, applications, and communication channels, and permeates everything we do. Take wireless and the different Internet standards and protocols that are being developed, the software crosses boundaries. Software is what makes wireless devices work. Software is what makes Web sites work. Software is what makes internal corporate operations happen, so software has become the glue that holds a lot of technologies together.

Right now the technologies that are high in demand are Java, object oriented design and development experience, Web development—how to build Web pages, how to write, and how to actually program Web sites are good skills. It's more than just presenting content to a user.

Another important skill is with respect to databases. Databases are still the foundation for pretty much all software at this point. Most applications are still very much data driven. High-tech candidates need to be grounded in these base technologies, but the more important skill set to have is good engineering expertise and knowing how to actually translate an idea into a project and executing the project.

Being a good communicator and working with teams are needed because the interpersonal issues, project management, and business skills are the ones that make those experiences and those technical skills important. Hig-tech employees have to be strong in both, and again, the more senior somebody wants to get, the more they need to be able to leverage their technology skills with communication and business skills.

Daniel Jaye, Engage, CTO & Cofounder

The Varying Roles of the CTO

A lot of it depends on the talent pool of the executive team. If the team has strong engineering management, the CTO doesn't necessarily have to be as involved with guiding the specific delivery of technologies, and can focus more on ensuring that the technology solutions are best of breed, the highest quality, innovative, and customer focused. In other companies it may be appropriate given the skill set of the management team for the CTO to have a more operational role. Typically, though, the CTO of a mature company is somewhat separated from that operational role, and is more focused on ensuring that the company is delivering the best quality technology solutions in the market—solutions that are going to take the company where it needs to be in the future.

Key Skills to Look for in a Tech Candidate

Problem-solving ability is probably the first and foremost skill to look for in a candidate for a tech team. Second of all is domain expertise; start off with a core of senior people who have been there, done that. Look for people who are going to be able to work together; there are many talented people in the industry, but sometimes talent comes with an inability to work as part of a team. Companies get better results and secondary benefits, such as better morale and a better culture and environment for working, when they have people who are not only extremely talented but also balanced individuals who work well as part of a team and with others, and embody principles like mutual respect, mentorship, etc.

There are a couple of strategic points for acquiring people with these kinds of attributes. One is that we are fortunate enough to have a great pool of people in the company today with these resources, and we do what we can to make sure that they're very happy with what they're doing, because they are our greatest asset. I have been able to attract top quality talent with those skills in the past, but it really comes down to working with the independent recruiters and with the candidates directly to really try to focus on people who are athletes. We want people with good strong skills, and are not necessarily after people strictly on the basis of what company they worked for last.

Gordon Caplan, Esq., Mintz Levin Strategies

The Most Important Components of an Employment Contract

As an employer, the most important thing to have is the ability to terminate without cause and without a significant penalty. Employers often think employment agreements are good for them, but that's not necessarily the case. We often advise clients that they should stay away from employment agreements and instead have non-disclosure and non-compete agreements.

The other important issue, especially from an intellectual property perspective, is to have a good work-for-hire provision that clearly states who owns the stuff going on in people's heads and being developed while they're at work or within the scope of their employment for the employers. That's something that is often missed and there's a lot of focus on non-competition but not enough focus on work-for-hire arrangements.

Employees often don't get good counsel, because they don't want to spend the money. They don't want to spend time on defining what they do get and what they don't get in the form of equity and/or more traditional cash compensation in the event that they're terminated for any reason. It could be a termination because of a disability or death or more likely just a termination by resignation or firing. Employees don't focus enough on defining the "cause and not for cause" and that's an important thing for employees to make sure they're getting good advice on.

Bonnie Hochman & Harrison Smith, Krooth & Altman

Basics of the Employment Relationship

The process of building and growing a company involves a range of critical challenges. As you focus your energies on raising funding and getting your products to market, one of the most critical challenges for the long-term growth and success of your company may be overlooked—the need to find, hire and retain the very best employees. You need to structure the relationship between your company and its employees in a way that will help you attain those goals while at the same time protecting your company from employee litigation and liability. Additionally, you need to plan for the inevitable future loss of employees, either due to voluntary turnover or enforced termination.

Your employment planning and structure needs to address the three stages of the employment relationship: 1) interviewing and hiring; 2) employment; and 3) the termination of the relationship. Let's examine each of these issues in turn.

I. Interviewing and Hiring

A. The Importance of Properly Screening Applicants for Employment

Mistakes in the hiring process, regrettably, are the origin of much of the employment litigation that is pervading today. Who, when, and how to hire employees is actually one of the most important decisions a company can make. In formulating your hiring strategies, you should carefully consider the following issues:

Prior to advertising or hiring for a position, it is generally useful to conduct a needs assessment;

Before hiring, your company should prepare a job description for each position;

Your advertisement soliciting candidates or your direction to your placement firm should state the essential functions of jobs and include a statement that your company does not discriminate;

Each representative from your company who will be interviewing candidates should be trained concerning proper interview questions and techniques;

Your employment application should be updated regularly and reviewed to ensure compliance with all legal requirements;

Your company's pre-employment inquiries should ask only job-related questions and omit any questions that may be viewed as discriminatory;

Your employment application process should serve to properly screen all applicants (i.e., you should verify work history, making sure that any gaps in employment are explained, verify licenses and degrees, and contact prior employers for references);

You should conduct a criminal background check and/or other appropriate background checks in view of the nature of the job;

If you are using employment contracts, they should be regularly updated and reviewed;

It may be prudent to have your applicants certify that the information given in the application process is accurate, and include a statement to the effect that any misrepresentation is ground for termination or for not offering employment;

You should require applicants to give written authorization for conducting reference checks and ensure compliance with the Fair Credit Reporting Act.

B. Discrimination in The Hiring Process

Various provisions of law prohibit a prospective employer from improperly discriminating in making hiring decisions.

For example, Title VII of the Civil Rights Act of 1964 prohibits discrimination against any individual on the basis of race, color, sex, national origin, or religion; the Age Discrimination in Employment Act (ADEA) protects prospective employees over the age of forty; and the American with Disabilities Act (ADA) protects applicants with disabilities. In some states it is illegal to discriminate against an employee based upon his or her sexual preference, marital status, weight, appearance, etc.

In order to comply with the various anti-discrimination laws, it is important that your hiring decisions be based solely on an applicant's suitability for a particular position and on that individual's qualifications alone. You must make your hiring decision without considering any of the prohibited class attributes (i.e. race, color, sex, national origin, religion, age, or disability. Note, however that under the ADA you may consider the extent to which the disability will interfere with the applicant's ability to perform essential job functions without the aid of reasonable accommodation.) Therefore, to protect yourself against allegations that you considered improper applicant attributes, you should refrain from soliciting any information (through an application or interview) that may raise the slightest hint of impropriety with respect to the hiring of an applicant.

C. Non-Competition and Non-Disclosure Agreements

Increasingly, non-competition agreements and non-disclosure agreements are becoming the rule rather than the exception in the realm of the hiring employees (especially high-tech.) In hiring a new employee you must make certain that the employee is not subject to any such agreements. Failure to do so may expose you to claims of interference by the job applicant's prior employer.

Non-competition agreements and non-disclosure agreements are both intended to protect a former employer's business by prohibiting its employees from leaving the company and making use of information, contacts and/or experience gained on the job. Each form of agreement works slightly differently. A non-disclosure agreement prohibits the employee from disclosing identified company information during and after employment. Such information will generally include broadly defined categories of information which the company deems to be important to the conduct of its business, such as trade secrets, customers, terms of sales, product designs, pending initiatives, etc. A non-competition agreement goes beyond a nondisclosure agreement and prohibits an employee from competing with a former employer either by taking a job with a competitor or by going into business on his or her own.

Both types of agreements restrict your ability to hire a new employee and additionally restrict that employee's ability to use their knowledge and experience on your behalf. Hence, when hiring an employee, you must inquire as to whether the prospective employee is restricted by the non-competition or non-disclosure agreement of a previous employer. You should inquire as to the specific terms of any such agreements, determine whether your hiring of the applicant and their contemplated duties will violate such agreement and obtain assurances from the employee that it is in full compliance with such agreements.

You may be able to circumvent a pre-existing non-competition agreement by showing that it is illegal and unenforceable. The inquiry in most jurisdictions turns on whether the agreement or covenant unfairly restricts the employee from continuing his or her livelihood after the termination of employment. In determining whether a non-competition agreement is valid, courts often analyze the duration and scope of the agreement. For instance, a non-competition agreement cannot prohibit an employee from working in a particular field for an unreasonable period of time. Similarly, a covenant not to compete cannot consist of unreasonable geographic limitations. In these instances, courts will often eliminate the unreasonable restrictions and permit the employee to compete directly with a former employer or disseminate the former employer's trade secrets.

D. Unethical Recruiting (and Anti-Solicitation Agreements)

In today's job market, many employers rely increasingly on their employees to assist in recruitment, often soliciting friends and associates from their former positions. In response, many employment contracts now contain prohibitions against the solicitation of former coworkers. If you actively encourage your new (and prospective) employees to solicit and recruit their coworkers, you may be held liable for intentional interference with such contractual relationships or you may be charged with civil conspiracy. Accordingly, you should carefully contemplate how you advertise job openings and whether to rely on the assistance of your employees.

II. Employment

A. Employment-at-Will

In the absence of an express contractual employment agreement between you and the employee, the employment relationship is governed by the tenet of employment-at-will. Under the doctrine of employment-at-will, both you and the employee have the right to terminate the employment relationship at any time and for any reason subject to federal regulations (e.g., Title VII, ADEA, or ADA) and public policy. However, this aged principal, premised in theory on the equality of rights, has been diluted by the courts, which have been willing to imply the existence of an employment agreement based upon various aspects of the interaction between employer and employee, such as the terms of an employee handbook.

B. Provisions to Include in Employment Agreements

In addition to providing certainty by setting forth terms of employment, compensation schemes, and benefit plans, employment contracts may be valuable in protecting your business ideas, client lists, and other confidential and proprietary information. Employment agreements may be as simple as a one-paragraph agreement setting forth the duration and salary of the job or may be several pages long encompassing expectations and obligations. While you will need to determine what type of agreement suits your requirements you may want to consider properly tailored covenants-not-to-compete, confidentiality provisions, and methods for resolving disputes (i.e. jurisdictional requirements, alternative dispute mechanisms such as arbitration, etc.).

C. Employee Handbooks and Their Impact on Employment-at-Will

While not all businesses benefit from employee handbooks, employee handbooks provide a forum for you to communicate with your employees on a number of policies such as employee behavior, disciplinary procedures, compensation schedules as well as information on benefits, leave, and vacation. In short, not only do employee handbooks allow you to implement consistent supervisory policies for the benefit of your employees, but the handbooks also provide your employees with definitive guidelines regarding those policies. Regardless of the size of your business, you may be able to benefit by having an employee handbook so long as you are dedicated to complying with its content. Such handbooks can cover issues such as leave (medical, vacation, bereavement, holidays, or other) policies, confidentiality issues, covenants-not-to-compete, sexual harassment and discrimination prohibitions, benefit plans and insurance, performance reviews, dress codes, client relations, company ethics, disciplinary actions and procedures, and even weather closings. Indeed, depending upon the nature and size of your business, employee handbooks can be quite beneficial in expressing a broad range of policy and procedure.

Because handbooks often detail procedures and policies, deviation from those set forth in the handbooks can be worse than having no definite procedure or policy in the first instance. In recent years courts have increasingly viewed employee handbooks as more than simply an expression of policy and instead as contractual in nature. Indeed, courts have bypassed a fundamental tenet of contract law by permitting employee handbooks to serve as unilateral contractual arrangements that can potentially bind employers to the policies set forth therein. The end result of this trend in the judicial construction of employee handbooks is deterioration in the long-standing doctrine of employment-at-will.

As a result of this transformation of employee handbooks and personnel manuals from merely gratuitous expressions of employer policy to an enforceable legal obligation, you may find yourself bound by and unable to change or escape your very own employee handbook. Indeed, employees are successfully using employee handbooks offensively to restrict employers from exercising their customary level of supervisory freedom in the workplace.

To limit the employee's ability to utilize the employee handbook as a mechanism for rights not specifically contemplated or expressly agreed upon by your company, you can employ a number of preventive measures. These preventive measures include a clear and concise disclaimer indicating that the employment relationship is an employment at will relationship and that the existence of the handbook does not create any contractual rights between the parties, an acknowledgment form indicating the employee's acknowledgment of the disclaimer as well as carefully wording the language in the employee handbook. In short, you should "say what you mean" and "mean what you say" when drafting an employee handbook.

D. Family and Medical Leave Act Requirements

The Family and Medical Leave Act (FMLA) went into effect in 1993 to require employers with 50 or more employees to provide up to 12 weeks per year of unpaid family and medical leave to eligible employees and to restore those employees to the same or an equivalent position upon their return. The FMLA allows eligible employees (male or female) to take leave for the birth, adoption, or placement in foster care of a child; the care of a seriously ill child, spouse, or parent; or the employee's own serious illness. While the FMLA only governs about 5 percent of all businesses (those with more than 50 employees), many states have their own family and medical leave laws, which are more comprehensive. For example, the District of Columbia has one of the broadest such laws entitling eligible employees (of employers with 20 or more employees) to up to 16 weeks of unpaid family leave and 16 weeks of unpaid medical leave during any 24-month period. Eligibility and thresholds vary from state to state and go beyond the scope of this article. However, you should keep in mind that as your company expands you may be obligated to permit employees leave for family and medical reasons and you may be obligated to hold open your employee's positions for certain periods of absences.

III. Termination of the Employment Relationship

Termination of an employment relationship, either by dismissal or by resignation, raises two concerns. First, more frequently than ever, employees are seeking legal redress of alleged improper firing and the employer needs to be prepared. The simplest way to protect against claims of improper dismissal is to deal directly and consistently with your employees. Enforce consistent standards or performance; document employee transgressions; and inform employees of failures of performance.

The second major concern involved in the termination of an employment relationship is the employer's concern that the former employee will act against the interests of the employer by competing, disclosing trade secrets, or otherwise. The best way to avoid this problem is by employing exit interviews to inform employees of the agreements to which they are bound and entering into termination agreements reinforcing those agreements.

A. Termination of the At-Will-Employment Relationship

As detailed earlier, the general rule of law in most jurisdictions is that private employers are free to discharge at-will employees (employees not bound by an employment contract) for good cause, for no cause or even for a morally wrong cause without facing liability, unless such cause is prohibited by law (i.e. Title VII, ADA, or ADEA). Likewise, employees are generally free to terminate the employment relationship at will as well. Some employers require written notice prior to termination by either party.

B. Termination of Employees With Employment Agreements

If you enter into an employment agreement with your employees, they cease to be at-will employees and their employment, including termination, is subject to the terms of the employment contract. This is true both in the case of an express agreement and in the case of an implied agreement based, for example, upon your employee handbook. Thus, always review your employment agreements prior to any terminations to ensure that you comply with any contractual agreements.

C. Termination of the Employment Relationship Through Constructive Discharge

You may terminate an employee without expressly doing so. An employer may not avoid the rules governing employee discharge by creating an intolerable work atmosphere that forces an employee to quit involuntarily. In order to give rise to a viable cause of action for constructive discharge, a court must find that the employee's working conditions were so difficult or unpleasant that a reasonable person in the employee's position would have also felt compelled to resign. Therefore, as this is an objective standard, an employee may not be unreasonably sensitive to his or her working environment as courts will not permit an employee's subjective perceptions to govern the claim. For instance, the employee must substantiate that his or her supervisors engaged in a pattern of baseless criticism, threatened termination, arbitrary treatment, overworking the employee, or yelling at an employee in front of others.

The simplest way for you to protect yourself from a potential claim of constructive discharge is to monitor your workplace and assure that conditions that could be construed as a constructive discharge are not permitted to exist. Additionally, to the extent you can deal with employees one on one (as opposed to in front of a department or group), you will protect yourself from a potential constructive discharge claim based on an unpleasant working environment. If you need to discharge an employee, do it directly, documenting instances of an employee's insubordination or failure to perform the assigned work adequately. By establishing a detailed record of non-performance, the employee will have a difficult time proving that any criticism or threat of termination was unfounded.

D. Limitations on the Right to Fire

1. Title VII, ADA, and ADEA

As detailed above, these statutes prohibit discrimination against any individual on the basis of race, color, sex, national origin, religion, age, or disability. If you violate the prescriptions of these statutes, you risk substantial exposure from potential litigation as not only do these statutes permit compensatory and punitive damages but they also permit a prevailing plaintiff to recover attorney's fees.

Under modern day discrimination analysis an employee who belongs to a protected group can prove discrimination by either offering direct evidence of discriminatory intent or by establishing that the employer treated the employee less favorably than members of other groups without a legitimate reason for such difference. Because discrimination by direct evidence is difficult for many employees to prove, the modern statutory framework permits an employee to prove discrimination by inference in the absence of direct evidence. Thus, if an employee can prove that he or she is a member of a protected class and suffered an adverse action that an employee outside of his or her protected class has not suffered, the employee will have established a prima facie case of discrimination and the burden then shifts to the employer to establish that the adverse action was the result of a legitimate business decision. If the employer can so establish, the burden shifts back to the employee to prove that the alleged legitimate business decision was simply a pre-text for discrimination.

The best defense against a potential claim of discriminatory firing is to ensure that there is a legitimate and well-documented business rationale for each employment decision. It is permissible to terminate someone in a protected class as long as the termination stems from performance or other legitimate business concerns and not purely from the employee belonging to that protected class.

2. Worker Adjustment Retraining and Notification Act (WARN)

As a result of numerous mergers and acquisitions in the late 1980s, Congress passed the Worker Adjustment Retraining and Notification Act (WARN). Under WARN, an affected employer generally cannot order a plant closing or mass layoff until 60 days after it serves proper notice to: 1) an authorized union for the affected employees; 2) each affected employee if there is no union; or 3) the dislocated worker unit. Employers who fail to comply with the 60 days' notice requirement of WARN will potentially face fines and civil liability, including liability for all wages and benefits for the affected employees for the period of the violation, up to 60 days.

Pursuant to the regulations, WARN applies to all profit and non-profit corporations (as well as governmental agencies engaged in a commercial enterprise) that employ 100 or more employees (not including part-time employees) or 100 or more employees who work in total of at least 4,000 hours per week (excluding overtime.) Independent contractors and subsidiaries may be treated as employees depending on their degree of independence from the contracting or parent company.

E. Issues You Should Consider Upon the Termination of the Employment Relationship (By You or the Employee)

1. Return of Various Materials

In the event that the employment relationship comes to an end, you must protect yourself from the possibility of theft, the sharing of trade secrets, or the employee going into competition with you or soliciting your clients for their new employer. Accordingly, in order to minimize any potential of wrongdoing or infringement upon the operation of your company, you should take these several important steps:

1) Obtain all company property from the employee;

2) Retake possession of all company credit cards, calling cards, handbooks, and files from the employee;

3) Ensure that the employee does not transmit or hold on to any confidential information regarding past, current, or prospective clients;

4) Collect all keys (and change the locks if necessary) to protect against future re-entry by the employee; and

5) Eliminate the employee's potential of accessing the system or shared network for the company.

By taking these few simple steps, you will limit any potential liability or damage that may result from the termination of the employment relationship by you or the employee.

2. Exit Interviews and Termination Agreements

In the case of either firing or resignation, use an exit interview and a termination agreement to protect your interests. This is your opportunity to clarify with the employee your expectation of their obligations pursuant to non-competition agreements, non-disclosure agreements, anti-solicitation agreements, etc. A termination agreement may also set forth the reasons for the termination of the employment agreement and may provide evidence that the termination was voluntary on the part of the employee or legitimate on the part of the employer, thus preventing future litigation by the employee.

In the event that you have not previously obtained adequate non-disclosure agreements, non-competition agreements, anti-solicitation agreements, etc., you may be able to do so at this point. It is not uncommon for the employer and the employee to have various final details to document and this negotiation may provide an opportunity to strengthen your protections in these areas. In addition, terminated employees may be receiving severance payments, adding to their incentive to agree to reasonable protections for you in these areas.

3. Settling the Employee's Last Paycheck

In the event the employee has an outstanding paycheck, depending upon your jurisdiction, you generally must provide your employee with that check within the course of the normal pay period. It is unlawful to withhold an employee's check for a period of time that is not congruent with what they would normally expect under your corporation's pay structure. Additionally, if the employee has outstanding financial obligations to your corporation, you may not exercise "self-help" and retain the money owed from the distributed paychecks. Courts are holding that employers have no greater standing to collect debts owed from their former employees than other creditors, i.e. you must settle these matters as part of your termination agreement or take later action against the former employee.

4. Blackballing (References)

A dilemma often faced by a former employer of a terminated employee is what to say, if anything, to a prospective employer seeking a referral or reference. Distilled to its essence, an employer may not prevent an employee from obtaining other employment or make misrepresentations to a prospective employer with the sole intent of preventing employment. If you "blackball" a former employee when providing a prospective employer with a reference, you risk a potential defamation lawsuit.

In light of the risk of a disgruntled employee filing a defamation lawsuit against a former employer, you are protected by a qualified privilege. With a qualified privilege, you are permitted to give a prospective employer honest information as to the character of the former employee—even if the assessment is inaccurate. To invoke the qualified privilege, you must simply attempt to furnish the job reference in good faith. Additionally, the person to whom the reference was furnished must have a legitimate interest or right to know the subject of the communication.

Given the current status of the law, you should play it safe and implement a policy that only provides prospective employers with the date of employment and salary information. By limiting the information provided to a prospective employer, you will substantially reduce the risk of litigation by a former employee.

IV. Conclusion

By considering the information contained in this primer regarding the basics of the employment relationship, you will equip yourself with a few basic tools to prevent and combat common employment disputes. The best defense to potential litigation is to proactively address problems before they arise. By staying a step ahead, you will find that, in the long run, you will save yourself from the costs and wasted time associated with frivolous litigation.

ASPATORE
BUSINESS REVIEW

The Quarterly Journal Featuring Exclusive Business Intelligence, Research & Analysis From Industry Insiders

Enabling Executives to Innovate & Outperform

The Most Subscribed to Publication of its Kind By C-Level Executives From the World's 100 Largest Companies

Only $1,090 a Year for 4 Comprehensive Issues

Aspatore Business Review brings you the most important, condensed business intelligence from industry insiders on a range of different topics affecting every executive, expanding your breadth of knowledge and enabling you to innovate and outperform.

Aspatore Business Review is the only way for business professionals to keep their edge and stay on top of the most pressing business issues. Each *Aspatore Business Review* features business intelligence, research and analysis from C-Level (CEO, CTO, CMO, CFO, Partner) executives, venture capitalists, investment bankers, lawyers, and analysts from the world's largest companies. Each quarterly issue focuses on the most pressing business issues, trends, and emerging opportunities in the marketplace that affect every industry in some way or another. Every quarter, *Aspatore Business Review* focuses on topics that every business professional needs to be aware of such as:

- Staying Ahead of Changing Markets
- Profiting in a Recession/Market Upswing
- Emerging Market Opportunities
- New Legal Developments
- Investment Banking Perspectives
- Management and Leadership
- Fostering Innovation
- Brand Building
- Economy Trends
- Stock Market Outlook
- Technology and the Internet
- Venture Capital Perspectives

Aspatore Business Review is the one publication every business professional should read, and is the best way to maintain your edge and keep current with your business reading in the most time efficient manner possible.

Fill Out the Order Form on the Other Side or Visit Us Online!
www.Aspatore.com

ASPATORE BUSINESS REVIEW
Tear Out This Page and Mail or Fax To:

Aspatore Books, PO Box 883, Bedford, MA 01730
Or Fax To (617) 249-1970

Name:

Email:

Shipping Address:

City: State: Zip:

Billing Address:

City: State: Zip:

Phone:

Lock in at the Current Rates Today-Rates Increase Every Year
Please Check the Desired Length Subscription:

1 Year ($1,090) _____   2 Years (Save 10%-$1,962) _____
5 Years (Save 20%-$4,360) _____   10 Years (Save 30%-$7,630) _____
Lifetime Subscription ($24,980) _____

(If mailing in a check you can skip this section but please read fine print below and sign below)
Credit Card Type (Visa & Mastercard & Amex):

Credit Card Number:

Expiration Date:

Signature:

Would you like us to automatically bill your credit card at the end of your subscription so there is no discontinuity in service? (You can still cancel your subscription at any point before the renewal date.) Please circle: Yes   No

*(Please note the billing address much match the address on file with your credit card company exactly)

Terms & Conditions
We shall send a confirmation receipt to your email address. If ordering from Massachusetts, please add 5% sales tax on the order (not including shipping and handling). If ordering from outside of the US, an additional $51.95 per year will be charged for shipping and handling costs. All issues are paperback and will be shipped as soon as they become available. Sorry, no returns or refunds at any point unless automatic billing is selected, at which point you may cancel at any time before your subscription is renewed (no funds shall be returned however for the period currently subscribed to). Issues that are not already published will be shipped upon publication date. Publication dates are subject to delay-please allow 1-2 weeks for delivery of first issue. If a new issue is not coming out for another month, the issue from the previous quarter will be sent for the first issue. For the most up to date information on publication dates and availability please visit www.Aspatore.com.

ORDER THESE OTHER GREAT BOOKS TODAY!
Great for Yourself or Your Entire Team
Visit Your Local Bookseller Today!

Bigwig Briefs: Management & Leadership (ISBN: 1587620146)
Industry Experts Reveal the Secrets How to Get There, Stay There, and Empower Others That Work For You

Bigwig Briefs: Management & Leadership includes knowledge excerpts from some of the leading executives in the business world. These highly acclaimed executives explain how to break into higher ranks of management, how to become invaluable to your company, and how to empower your team to perform to their utmost potential.

Bigwig Briefs: The Golden Rules of the Internet Economy (ISBN: 1587620138)
Industry Experts Reveal the Best Advice Ever on Succeeding in the Internet Economy

Bigwig Briefs: The Golden Rules of the Internet Economy includes knowledge excerpts from some of the leading business executives in the Internet and Technology industries. These highly acclaimed executives explain where the future of the Internet economy is heading, mistakes to avoid for companies of all sizes, and the keys to long term success.

Bigwig Briefs: Startups Keys to Success (ISBN: 1587620170)
Industry Experts Reveal the Secrets to Launching a Successful New Venture

Bigwig Briefs: Startups Keys to Success includes knowledge excerpts from some of the leading VCs, CEOs CFOs, CTOs and business executives in every industry. These highly acclaimed executives explain the secrets behind the financial, marketing, business development, legal, and technical aspects of starting a new venture.

Bigwig Briefs: Guerrilla Marketing (ISBN: 1587620677)
The Best of Guerrilla Marketing

Best selling author Jay Levinson shares the now world famous principles behind guerrilla marketing, in the first ever "brief" written on the subject. Items discussed include the Principles Behind Guerrilla Marketing, What Makes a Guerrilla, Attacking the Market, Everyone Is a Marketer, Media Matters, Technology and the Guerrilla Marketer, and Dollars and Sense. A must have for any big time marketing executive, small business owner, entrepreneur, marketer, advertiser, or any one interested in the amazing, proven power of guerrilla marketing.

Bigwig Briefs: Small Business Internet Advisor (ISBN: 1587620189)
Industry Experts Reveal the Secrets to Internet Marketing, BizDev, HR, Financing, eCommerce and Other Important Topics Facing Every Small Business Doing Business on the Internet

Bigwig Briefs: Small Business Internet Advisor includes knowledge excerpts from some of the leading executives in the world in every field of specialty. These highly acclaimed executives explain the secrets behind making the most of your small business online in a very easy to understand and straight forward fashion.

Bigwig Briefs: Term Sheets & Valuations (ISBN: 1587620685)
A Detailed Look at the Intricacies of Term Sheets & Valuations

Bigwig Briefs: Term Sheets & Valuations is the first ever in-depth look at the nuts and bolts of terms sheets and valuations. The book, written by leading venture capitalist Alexander Wilmerding of Boston Capital Ventures, covers topics such What is a Term Sheet, How to Examine a Term Sheet, A Section-by-Section View of a Term Sheet, Valuations, What Every Entrepreneur & Executive Needs to Know About Term Sheets, Valuation Parameters, and East Coast Versus West Coast Rules. In addition, the book includes an actual term sheet from a leading law firm with line by line descriptions of each clause, what can/should be negotiated, and the important points to pay attention to. A must have book for any executive, entrepreneur, or financial professional.

Inside the Minds: Venture Capitalists (ISBN: 1587620014)
Inside the High Stakes and Fast Paced World of Venture Capital - *Inside the Minds: Venture Capitalists* features leading partners from Softbank, ICG, Sequoia Capital, CMGI, New Enterprise Associates, Bertelsmann Ventures, TA Associates, Kestrel Venture Management, Blue Rock Capital, Novak Biddle Venture Partners, Mid-Atlantic Venture Funds, Safeguard Scientific, Divine interVentures, and Boston Capital Ventures. Learn how some of the best minds behind the Internet revolution value companies, assess business models, and identify opportunities in the marketplace.

Inside the Minds: Leading Marketers (ISBN: 1587620537)
Industry Leaders Share Their Knowledge on the Future of Marketing, Advertising and Building Successful Brands - *Inside the Minds: Leading Marketers* features leading CMOs/EVPs of marketing from General Electric, Federal Express, Coke, Yahoo!, Ford, American Express, Verizon, Major League Baseball and Best Buy. These leading marketers share their knowledge on the future of the marketing industry, the everlasting effects of the Internet and technology, guerrilla marketing, best marketing for the dollars, public relations, advertising, building and sustaining a brand, and other important topics.

Inside the Minds: Chief Technology Officers (ISBN: 1587620081)
Industry Experts Reveal the Secrets to Developing, Implementing, and Capitalizing on the Best Technologies in the World - *Inside the Minds: Chief Technology Officers* features leading technology executives from companies such as Engage, Datek, Symantec, Verisign, Vignette, WebMD, SONICblue, Kana Communications, Flooz.com and The Motley Fool. Their experiences, advice, and research provide an unprecedented look at the various strategies involved with developing, implementing, and capitalizing on the best technologies in the world for companies of every size and in every industry.

Inside the Minds: The Wireless Industry (ISBN: 1587620200)
Industry Leaders Discuss the Future of the Wireless Revolution - *Inside the Minds: The Wireless Industry* features leading CEOs from companies such as AT & T Wireless, Omnisky, Wildblue, AirPrime, Digital Wireless, Aperto Networks, Air2Web, LGC Wireless, Arraycomm, Informio and Extenta. Items discussed include the future of the wireless industry, wireless devices, killer-apps in the wireless industry, the international landscape, government issues and more.

Inside the Minds: Leading Women (ISBN: 1587620197)
What it Takes for Women to Succeed and Have it All in the 21st Century - *Inside the Minds: Leading Women* features CEOs and executives from companies such as Prudential, Women's Financial Network, SiliconSalley.com, Barclays Global Investors, RealEco.com, AgentArts, Kovair, MsMoney.com, LevelEdge and AudioBasket. These

highly acclaimed women explain how to balance personal and professional lives, set goals, network, start a new company, learn the right skills for career advancement and more.

Inside the Minds: Leading Advertisers (ISBN: 1587620545)
Industry Leaders Share Their Knowledge on the Future of Building Brands Through Advertising – *Inside the Minds: Leading Advertisers* features CEOs/Presidents from agencies such as Young & Rubicam, Leo Burnett, Ogilvy, Saatchi & Saatchi, Interpublic Group, Valassis, Grey Global Group and FCB Worldwide. These leading advertisers share their knowledge on the future of the advertising industry, the everlasting effects of the Internet and technology, client relationships, compensation, building and sustaining brands, and other important topics.

Inside the Minds: Leading Consultants (ISBN: 1587620596)
Industry Leaders Share Their Knowledge on the Future of the Consulting Profession and Industry - *Inside the Minds: Leading Consultants* features leading CEOs/Managing Partners from some of the world's largest consulting companies. These industry leaders share their knowledge on the future of the consulting industry, being an effective team player, the everlasting effects of the Internet and technology, compensation, managing client relationships, motivating others, teamwork, the future of the consulting profession and other important topics.

Inside the Minds: Leading CEOs (ISBN: 1587620553)
Industry Leaders Share Their Knowledge on Management, Motivating Others, and Making a Difference At Any Level Within an Organization - *Inside the Minds: Leading CEOs* features some of the biggest name, proven CEOs in the world. These highly acclaimed CEOs share their knowledge on management, the Internet and technology, client relationships, compensation, motivating others, building and sustaining a profitable business and making a difference at any level within an organization.

Inside the Minds: Internet Marketing (ISBN: 1587620022)
Industry Experts Reveal the Secrets to Marketing, Advertising, and Building a Successful Brand on the Internet - *Inside the Minds: Internet Marketing* features leading marketing VPs from some of the top Internet companies in the world including Buy.com, 24/7 Media, DoubleClick, Guerrilla Marketing, Viant, MicroStrategy, MyPoints.com, WineShopper.com, Advertising.com and eWanted.com. Their experiences, advice, and stories provide an unprecedented look at the various online and offline strategies involved with building a successful brand on the Internet for companies in every industry. Also examined is calculating return on investment, taking an offline brand online, taking an online brand offline, where the future of Internet marketing is heading, and numerous other issues.

Inside the Minds: Internet Bigwigs (ISBN: 1587620103)
Industry Experts Forecast the Future of the Internet Economy (After the Shakedown) - *Inside the Minds: Internet Bigwigs* features executives from Excite (Founder), Beenz.com (CEO), Organic (CEO), Agency.com (Founder), Egghead (CEO), Credite Suisse First Boston (Internet Analyst), CIBC (Internet Analyst) and Sandbox.com. Items discussed include killer-apps for the 21st century, the stock market, emerging industries, international opportunities, and a plethora of other issues affecting anyone with a "vested interest" in the Internet and technology revolution.

Other Best Selling Business Books Include:

Bigwig Briefs: Become a CEO
Bigwig Briefs: Become a VP of Marketing
Bigwig Briefs: Become a CTO
Bigwig Briefs: Become a VP of BizDev
Bigwig Briefs: Become a CFO
Bigwig Briefs: The Art of Deal Making
Bigwig Briefs: Career Options for Law School Students
Bigwig Briefs: Career Options for MBAs
Bigwig Briefs: Online Advertising
Bigwig Briefs: Term Sheets & Valuations
Bigwig Briefs: Venture Capital
Inside the Minds: Leading Accountants
Inside the Minds: Leading CTOs
Inside the Minds: Leading Deal Makers
Inside the Minds: Leading Wall St. Investors
Inside the Minds: Leading Investment Bankers
Inside the Minds: Internet BizDev
Inside the Minds: Internet CFOs
Inside the Minds: Internet Lawyers
Inside the Minds: The New Health Care Industry
Inside the Minds: The Financial Services Industry
Inside the Minds: The Media Industry
Inside the Minds: The Real Estate Industry
Inside the Minds: The Automotive Industry
Inside the Minds: The Telecommunications Industry
OneHourWiz: Becoming a Techie
OneHourWiz: Stock Options
OneHourWiz: Public Speaking
OneHourWiz: Making Your First Million
OneHourWiz: Internet Freelancing
OneHourWiz: Personal PR & Making a Name For Yourself
OneHourWiz: Landing Your First Job
OneHourWiz: Internet & Technology Careers (After the Shakedown)

Go to www.Aspatore.com for a Complete List of Titles!

ASPATORE BOOKS